MODERN
SOCIAL
MOVEMENTS

STUDIES IN SOCIOLOGY

Consulting Editor

CHARLES H. PAGE

UNIVERSITY OF CALIFORNIA, SANTA CRUZ

MODERN
SOCIAL
MOVEMENTS

A Sociological Outline

Wm. Bruce Cameron

THE UNIVERSITY OF SOUTH FLORIDA

RANDOM HOUSE

NEW YORK

ACKNOWLEDGMENTS

I wish to acknowledge my debt to Richard Dewey and Gerard DeGré who first directed my attention to this area when I was their student at Butler University. In addition, I have profited from insights of some of my own students who are now active in the social sciences: Robert Carroll, Ray Cuzzort, Raymond Wheeler, Felix Moos, Sally Saulvester, Bertram Gardner, Adam Nazarko, Brother John Dundas, and others. I have read all of the systematic treatments of social movements I could find, and borrowed ideas liberally. Failure to mention many of these works in a small book should not be construed as criticism. I am pleased to include a description of the Negro Civil Rights movement by James Laue, and some salient quotations from a number of sources which are cited in the text. The enthusiasm and helpfulness of people interested in this field are such that I have collected far more material than these covers can contain. I can only offer to share informally with others to repay what I have received. Finally, I am pleased to express my gratitude to Russell M. Cooper and my secretary, Joann Dabbs, and most especially to Charles H. Page for his extensive editorial suggestions.

CONTENTS

MODERN
SOCIAL
MOVEMENTS

Introduction

SOCIAL MOVEMENTS

AS AN

AREA OF PROBLEMS

The best justification for studying anything is that we are interested in it. For readers who are not yet interested in social movements it may be desirable to offer some secondary reasons for such a study, relating social movements to more crucial phenomena in our lives, or perhaps regarding social movements as a means to some nobler, and self-justifying, end.

Men apparently become most concerned with problems of social control and social change precisely at those times when control is breaking up and the patterns of behavior are changing. Plato lived in the midst of political chaos. Hobbes, Locke, and Rousseau all witnessed political upheaval. Since the culture of any modern society seems likely to change, we might profitably study some of the processes by which changes occur, and social movements are one such process.

This book attempts to describe social movements within the scope of existing social theory. Admittedly, this has the disadvantage of often appearing overly general when talking about a specific occurrence, but it also allows us to interpret social movements in terms which are already familiar from studies of other social behav-

ior, while permitting us to use any specific insights we
gain from studying social movements when we deal
with other aspects of society.

The reader may of course question whether the characteristics ascribed to social movements do not apply
much more generally to many other social phenomena.
This is always a question with any theory. For example,
a colleague may severely criticize an article on the use of
marijuana on the ground that the principles set forth as
describing how a man learns to use marijuana are far
too general in that they explain equally well how one
learns to like ripe olives, or to play football. E. H. Suth-
erland's description of how one becomes a professional
thief underwent similar criticism, namely that the same
events and practices he described hold for lawyers, doctors, college professors, or indeed almost any profession.
The question is one of the degree of abstraction involved. If we abstract far enough, almost anything appears to be like almost anything else. If we remain sufficiently concrete, all things differ. As in many areas of
sociology, the study of social movements constantly
raises the twin questions of comparison: How are they
alike? and How do they differ?

Since little use has been made of the exact methods of
research so admirably employed by some other workers,
it would be presumptuous indeed to claim that this work
is definitive, or even systematic. The reader will find in
this book neither excellently established data nor a
tightly integrated theory organizing such data. Rather
he will find an account of some attributes which the
writer has found to be worth considering in trying to
gain an understanding of a number of specific movements. He will also find suggestions of relationships between attributes as seen in various movements. For sim-
plicity these may be stated dogmatically, but it should
be remembered that they are not absolutes. Indeed,
they may not even be general tendencies which could be
stated in terms of mathematical probability. They are
mostly naive correlations, apparent associations, and

even intuitive hunches which have not reached the stage of tightly formulated hypotheses. Although their form may be dogmatic, their function should be regarded as suggestive.

This does not fit the mathematical or scientific model of a theory, although some theoretical statements are made. Nor does it present a conclusion for policy, although persons who need to make policies may find suggestions in it. Its chief usefulness should lie in leading others to criticize the kind of description it permits, and to help them in further examining conflicting descriptions of social movements, and in reformulating their own notions of how social movements work. Thus, the significance of this book cannot lie in the book itself, but in what the reader does with it, and to it.

The bulk of the work of studying social movements lies outside this book. No complete concrete descriptions of particular social movements are presented, because the understanding of social movements does not consist in learning the facts about particular movements as seen by a particular sociologist or historian. Understanding lies, rather, in selecting a few you are interested in and studying them yourself, using this or some other guide in the beginning, and selectively developing a better one for yourself as you go along. The test of this or any other system of description and analysis, and the best source of knowledge and understanding, is to be sought in the field, directly observing and talking with the people who make up active social movements.

In short, this is not a text book, but essentially a study guide. It is an opening gambit in a game, an invitation to the reader to join in the process of looking at something he may find interesting and even important, and to join as a partner, not as an apprentice.

Chapter I

GENERAL

CHARACTERISTICS

Definition

This whole book is a kind of long definition of social movements with some appended references and some interspersed examples. The aim is to present a catalog of characteristics which enable a definition of any particular social movement. It falls short of this because any catalog must have many blank pages if it is to allow for the inclusion of things which are not yet created, and new social movements are being created all the time. Nor is all of this catalog of equal importance. Yet, with some sacrifice in precision and completeness, a short definition can be distilled out of it.

A social movement occurs when a fairly large number of people band together in order to alter or supplant some portion of the existing culture or social order.

To be sure, all of the important terms in this definition are ambiguous. I cannot state precisely what a "fairly large" number is. The nature of the "banding" is various and demands further scrutiny. The "portion of the culture" or of the "social order" is unspecified, as any aspect of human social life may be the target of some movement advocating change. However, even in such a general definition as this, discriminations have been made.

When we say that a movement "occurs" we recognize that the "thing" we are defining is not a material object which can be sensed at a particular moment but rather a procession of human behavior which takes place in time, and must be defined in temporal, as well as in spatial, terms. To readers used to thinking of mechanical objects, this observation may seem picayune, but it does characterize dynamic or changing phenomenon, and the essence of a social movement is change. I will later argue that some movements cease to exist essentially *because* they can no longer change the culture, or themselves, and that other movements change conditions around themselves so that they become no longer feasible or necessary.

The question of number is elusive, and does not lend itself to definitive statements. In our present society, movements exist partly because the individual can rarely produce the changes he desires solely by his own efforts, and he is forced to utilize the labors of others. How many others are required is impossible to state in the abstract, and often hard to determine even in specific historical contexts. Not all movements require the same sort of personal instrumentation, nor do all the individuals who make up a movement have equal value to it. Obviously some movements are too small to do the job they set out to do. Less obviously, some movements become too large. In the process of becoming larger, changes are forced upon the movement, and frequently it must make other changes in order to attract enough members to become large. However, despite the confusion in this question some meaningful statements can be made about the relation of size to the structure and success of social movements in general and the kinds of things they can and cannot do.

Part of the definition of anything consists of some notion of what it is not. Mere spatial mobility, for example, does not constitute a social movement, even though large numbers of people migrate together; nor does the moving about of a single person in society. These events belong more properly in other areas of sociological theory, especially in the study of population and social stratification. The interest here is in people changing culture, regardless of whether this involves changing their location or changing their social status. To be sure, anything which is generally true of society will be true of social movements, and questions about both status and mobility may be asked. Success of a movement does affect the statuses of its members, and often the initial status of its members foreordains the success. But while some movements must move spatially to succeed, transportation itself is not the key issue. The main characteristic of a social movement is that it seeks to change the culture or change the social structure or redistribute the power of control within a society.

Some writers have defined social movements as nearly synonymous with special kinds of organizational structure, such as political parties. Although many movements do take on this form, this is largely a historical accident in our recent experience. To limit the meaning of social movements to include only those movements which culminate in formal political action is to force too narrow a conception of man's history onto the data of his behavior.

It would appear then that there is no single necessary form which a movement must take. Some movements consist of tightly knit, intimate groups of persons who congregate in a small area and engage in almost constant direct communication. Others are made up of widely-scattered persons, who rarely if ever meet face to face. Many variations are encountered, and no single kind of organizational pattern need maintain for all members of the movement or for the movement throughout its entire life span. However, we should examine the forms and techniques of organization because different kinds of organization may serve more effectively to meet differing needs of movements and of individuals. As a rough generalization it may be said that movements seeking to deal effectively with a wide variety of persons and purposes must necessarily assume a varied organizational form.

Not all purposes of course are best instrumented by social movements, and not all changes in culture result from them. Many important social changes are unintended. We may well question the relative importance of technological and ideological innovations. In the next few years the most important changes in our culture may result less from the dreams of idealistic thinkers than from the anonymous work of researchers in the laboratories of Western Electric, Remington Rand, or other companies investigating electronic communication and control. The development of servo-mechanisms may well change our history more than all the exhortations of reformers put together.

Yet impressive as this is, it is not our purpose to examine it here. We are concerned only with deliberately planned changes brought about through social movements. All of man's activities have unforeseen consequences, but we are interested here in examining what some men do when they *deliberately* attempt to foresee and to direct changes in their culture.

Although social movements of various kinds have been occurring for a long time, they are of particular interest today. There is little need or call for social movements in a static society which successfully satisfies the felt wants of its members. Social change which is not accidental comes in response to dissatisfaction. But not all dissatisfactions everywhere give rise to social movements. The special conditions which do lead to the formation of social movements clearly include several factors: (1) Men must consciously recognize their dissatisfactions and share these with others. (2) Men must believe in their own ability to reshape the course of their lives. (3) Men must live under conditions in which the banding together to change something is both possible and plausibly effective.

In brief, the most likely habitat of a social movement is a democracy with easy communication in a state of unrest. It is in a democracy that men are most likely to look to themselves as the source of power for social change. Communication is essential if enough people are to share their similar dissatisfactions and find the numbers of kindred spirits to permit effective collective action. And there must be conditions of unrest to impel them to strike out on their own, against the current of immediate tradition, taking the chances that always go with being recognizably different, facing the risk of rebuff or even extermination which may at any time be the lot of the objecting minority. This is the picture of the "free world" today.

There are many ongoing social movements today, and the record of change attributable to some of these is impressive. For while in theory democracies obey the will of the majority, majorities often exercise no will, and a well organized minority may frequently substitute its will or impose it upon the majority. The awesome consequences of such political movements as Nazism and Communism have left too great a mark on our own lives for us to disregard social movements as mere collections of crackpots and malcontents. Malcontent they probably are, and more than a few disturbed personalities may be found in most social movements, but the effect and importance of a social movement cannot be judged by the characteristics and limitations of a few individual members.

The hard fact is that since some social movements have met with success in their efforts at change, others will take heart and try to follow their example. We cannot wish them away, nor can we ignore or exorcise them. We must try to understand them. And if we share the faith of scientists that there is regularity to be discovered in all of nature, including man's own behavior, then it behooves us to seek out the regularities in the phenomena of social movements and try to formulate principles by which these may be used and controlled.

To this end, we need to study all kinds of social movements, including both those we support and cherish and those we ardently despise. We must hold in check our emotional response to the purposes of these movements, lest we thereby obscure important facts. Just as a chess player must in imagination play his opponent's game, so too we must follow in our imagination the movement of our foe if we are to understand how best to form our own and how to combat his.

In order to discover the similarities of social movements we must compare many different kinds. And as they are not static objects which may be taken into a study or laboratory and placed side by side for scrutiny, we must content ourselves largely with abstractions of movements, presented in words. Description, again mostly in words, must precede analysis. But since analysis can only reveal similarities which are present in the descriptions, the descriptions themselves need to be made according to some uniform plan. The analysis is thus both facilitated and limited by the scheme of the descriptions.

In the beginning of such a study, the choice of characteristics is apt to be somewhat irrational and unplanned. Usually, one abstracts those characteristics which he finds most striking, those which he has previously found to be useful in dealing with other kinds of objects, and others which for various reasons "seem to belong." Analyzing what he has, he perceives that some of these fall into patterns, and may be subsumed under more general characteristics, some of which lead to finer distinctions and require more exact descriptions of characteristics, and many of which appear to lead to nothing at all. Armed with this information and these tentative hunches about the organization of the objects, he continues examining and describing more objects in order to check the notions he has developed, and so it goes. Such a task probably has no real end, although "conclusions" may be drawn at any point along the way, depending upon one's standards of precision, the model of statement, or the demand for practical policy.

At present the demand for practical policy-making is so great that many people seek immediately a formula sufficiently general to apply to widely diverse data, which will forcefully bring order into apparent chaos. The greater the desire for policy and the more confusing the data, the more avidly such a magical formula is sought. Some people may even grasp at bizarre formulations stated in vague but impressive language in a manner altogether inconsistent with the way in which they manage their everyday lives. One of the therapeutic aims of analysis, then, should be to reduce the characteristics of social movements which strike us immediately as weird, esoteric, and outlandish down to terms which through their familiarity appear merely pedestrian and commonplace. Part of the job of science is to make common and ordinary that which appears unusual and inscrutable.

This means that in our description of social movements we must begin by paying attention to some characteristics which are so simple and common that they may appear trivial. From an aesthetic standpoint, this may be regettable, since by so doing we may divest social movements of much of the glamor and terror they often present; but only when we can state clearly the simple things which we can dependably observe are we in a position to analyze the more subtle and devious developments. Moreover we will frequently find that once we do understand the more obvious facts about a movement the others seem to flow logically from these.

Numbers

A social movement involves a plurality of people. How many cannot be answered now apart from some other questions which are raised later, but the mere knowledge that a movement includes so-and-so many members makes it possible to infer some things which can be verified by observation.

First off, the size of groups naturally influences their intimacy—that willingness to reveal and share feelings and behavior with certain people which we do not show with most others. In other words, it means a condition of sympathy, mutual trust, and respect, in which we can "let down our hair," or "let down our guard," while feeling comparatively safe from exploitation, censure, or ridicule. Small groups may become intimate and often do, if some other conditions are met. Larger groups are less likely to become intimate, and beyond a certain size it is virtually impossible to achieve even a semblance of intimacy.

If half a dozen or a dozen people see each other often, they are apt to discuss other ideas besides those most central to the movement—love, food, sports, and all kinds of things which make up their lives. Merely in the course of living together they come to establish common meanings in many areas. This may continue to the point where often no deliberate effort at communication need be made—they simply "know" what the others are going to think, say, or do without having to ask or wonder. Thus from intimacy there may grow a special kind of consensus, in which each can look within his own thoughts and understand the thoughts of the other; in which each is so closely identified with the other that he agrees without even the possibility of differing, and where the points of agreement extend over a much wider area of life than the one with which the movement is explicitly concerned.

The possibility of intimacy or its lack presents a serious problem of choice for the founders of any social movement. A broad general consensus tends to increase the stability and continuity of the membership, but to insist upon it may restrict the size of the group to such a degree that the movement cannot achieve its purpose. To be sure, with such a consensus more purposes may be included, and included in an integrated, rather than a merely additive fashion, but practical considerations may lead them to relax the demand for consensus in order to attract people who share only one or a few of the group's objectives.

The founders of social movements are thus frequently ambivalent about an increase in size at the expense of intimate consensus, and devote much effort to finding compromises between these two qualities, both of which may be desirable. Sometimes the zeal for "purity" produces isolation from the general public, or even schisms within the movement, as can be seen in various stages of Communist history[1] and in most of the movements in the fine arts.

Since all movements must start with a few people, we may question whether the problem of size is not paramount in the formation of a social movement, particularly if we take political movements as the model. But it must be borne in mind that while political movements in a democracy ultimately need large numbers of people to put their programs into operation, many nonpolitical movements do not. The choice only arises pointedly when large numbers become necessary and not merely desirable. Many movements in art, literature, and other "symbolic" aspects of culture have satisfied their ends with a mere handful of members, although their influence was felt by a large part of the population in their time. Moreover this influence may continue in the general culture long after the members have died or dispersed to the extent that the movement itself is no longer recognizable.

This same issue may be discussed in terms of social control. Astute leaders and observers of social movements have stressed the importance of the disciplined minority, both as a form for the total movement and as a "hard core" which educates, mobilizes, and directs the "masses" of the larger movement when additional

[1] For a careful treatment of this theme, see Philip Selznick, *The Organizational Weapon*, New York: McGraw Hill, 1952.

partial-members are available and useful. The forms of control differ for different sized movements. In the small, intimate movement, informal controls are efficient. Members share most of the same ideas and attitudes, and respect each other as persons, and thus direct themselves and each other without formal machinery. A casual suggestion, or a personal plea, is probably the most effective means of control available, because through such means the person being controlled does not have the notion of control sharply thrown up to him. He does not feel that he is ordered, or compelled, but rather that he is appealed to and that he chooses to cooperate. If he can be persuaded to agree, and especially if he can assist in developing the policy himself, he actually controls himself. Self-control can thus be made the most congenial, and one of the surest forms, of social control.

But while informal control is the easiest to apply in a suitable situation, and can be applied whenever people meet, the presuppositions of intimacy, communication, and mutual respect which underly its success are not easily met. Indeed, when members number in the thousands they are rarely met; and more impersonal, formal machinery must be employed. Ironically, the very form of relationship which most effectively welds together the small nucleus of original members may severely handicap a larger group, and conversely, the machinery admirably suited to the needs of a large social movement may emasculate, devitalize, or obliterate a small one.

Thus leaders of growing social movements must attend closely to the subtle and gradual changes that occur as members are added. Obstinate adherence to a special form which was once suitable, or the personal inabilities of leaders to change their manner of operation even though they may recognize the need for change, may hamper social movements of all kinds. "The seeds of eventual destruction are often sown at the beginning."

As a general proposition we may assert that a social

movement which seeks to become large must include people with diverse interests, and include them on a segmental basis, so that each finds something within it, although few will be in total agreement with all policies and practices. The skillful combination of diverse elements in such a fashion that the main objectives can be realized at the expense of minor aims marks the successful large social movement. At the same time, large movements live in constant danger of dissolving into bickering factions should members focus their attention on the differences among them.

Purpose

We are concerned in this study with fairly large numbers of people who are bent on changing some part of their culture or, as the members of the movement see it, "improving" some part of that culture.

Social movements vary greatly as to the portion of the culture or the social order they attempt to change. Some are concerned with a very narrow segment of life. Some deal with a combination of several minor aspects. Some attack a major part of the culture, and in passing include changes in minor items which are related to it, either fortuitously or by logical necessity. And some movements are "totalitarian," attempting to control the whole social structure, and thereby virtually alter the entire culture.

Since there are no *a priori* limits to the purposes which a given movement might entertain, any classification of purposes must be somewhat arbitrary, and can be defended only on grounds of convenience. However, men themselves adopt certain handy classifications in viewing their own behavior, and some of these everyday pigeonholes provide a convenient starting point when trying to classify a movement.

For example, men in our society are frequently inclined to divide their behavior into such areas of life as religious, economic, and political. A thoroughgoing religionist might deplore any such division, maintaining that the ethical norms of religion should be applied every day in all behavior, whatever its context and intent, but the fact remains that few people do so. In a similar manner, we all know the stereotype of the economically oriented businessman who thinks of nothing but money and how to get it twenty-four hours a day, although in actual practice very few such men exist. Most of us in fact tend to live our lives in segments, seeing some relationships on one occasion, judging them with one set of values, and playing what we think is an appropriate role, and on another occasion employing different values and performing different roles.

So it is with social movements. Some movements are concerned with altering the religious life, others with the economic, and still others with the political, the artistic, the dietary, the educational, or the recreational. Since effective organization frequently requires that members of a movement devote much of their time and energy to a restricted purpose, this intensively specialized activity readily leads to misunderstandings with nonmembers. The average man, for example, regards animals as casual and minor members of the community; when he encounters someone whose life work is that of protecting cats and dogs from cruelty, he thinks the animal lover a bit queer, and may tell him so, while the anticruelty man angrily resents the other's crass unconcern and vigorously denounces his lack of conscience, his latent sadism, and perhaps also his lineage.

Generally, people in social movements take their movements, and themselves as members, much more seriously than do outsiders, with the result that in-group attitudes develop circularly. Contrast Mr. Average, for example, with a dedicated jazz musician. Mr. Average regards music as a pleasant addition to his dinner, the movies, or television commercials. When he feels happy, he may hum or whistle a tune, slightly off-key. He wants music when he dances—he does not dance very precisely to the music, but he would feel silly dancing with-

out it. In the cocktail bar, music soothes him, and fills in
the gaps in his conversation. He may attend a concert
once in a while, or buy phonograph records, and he likes
to hear the band at football games and during Veterans'
Day parades. Music is around him much of the time,
and he rather likes it. *Rather*—that is the rub. His is a
passive, aimless appreciation of many kinds of music
without critical attention to any of it.

The devout jazz musician, on the contrary, does not
"rather" like music. He loves it, some of it, with a con-
suming devotion that surpasses anything else, and he
hates some other types. Even to say that he loves music
is inaccurate, he lives it. Music is a vital part of his existence, the focus of his life. All of his tastes are geared to
music: his work, his sleep, his clothes, his friends; everything is colored and interpreted in terms of music.
Moreover, he is highly educated in this particular idiom,
and makes very fine critical distinctions in judging it—
just any music won't do. He is a man operating under a
driving compulsion to do something about music. Why
permit bad music when there can be "good"? He meets
a few others who share his tastes in what constitutes
good and bad music, and we have the birth of a movement. This brave little group is going to revolutionize
the way in which music is played. This will take a lot of
doing.

Now what this little cult actually does may not greatly
affect the public. Indeed, most of us may never hear of
them, and those of us who do may admire or resent their
efforts. Yet so far as these musicians themselves are concerned, this is not very significant, because they are too
wrapped up in their own concern to be able to take an
objective view of their own activities even if they
wished to do so. Living as they do, intently concerned
with a very small part of the total culture, they lose
touch with the rest of the world. When they do come
into contact with outsiders, the experiences are not satisfactory. The others don't know much about jazz, don't
care much about jazz, and prefer to talk about some-

thing else. Rebuffed, the musicians seek out their own kind, people who realize that jazz is the most important concern a man can have and who behave accordingly.

The description of this process can be ramified, but basically it goes like this: People with preferences find sympathy and friendship among others who share these preferences. They spend more time with their friends than with others, and the preferences become elaborated and sharpened. This puts them more out of step with the others, and when they perceive this, they retreat still more exclusively into the company of their friends, and so on. The result is isolation. Couple this with intense specialized interests, and we see the formation of a cult.

This is about as far as the movement of jazz musicians develops. They go their own way, occasionally scowling at the rest of us and pitying or ridiculing our insipid and infantile tastes, and we glare back at them in turn, but soon forget them. Each of us has more important matters to attend to.

Suppose, however, that the purpose around which a small group is united is political in nature, and that the effective instrumentation of this purpose would alter the structure of our government. To narrow it somewhat, suppose that the members regard military service as unjust, immoral, and unnecessary, and set out to eliminate everything military. Now, while many of us grumble at being drafted, and any veteran can offer some complaints about working for Uncle Sam, few of us would agree with this little group, especially about the unnecessary part. So when they haughtily insist that *they* cannot be drafted, we become more than a little annoyed. *We* are subject to being drafted, why shouldn't *they* be? They present reasons; we do not accept them; and both of us become loud and eventually violent. Police intervene in the discussion, and both public sentiment and statute law favor our side. We may be fined or warned to be more decorous in our behavior, if it is peace time, and may even be informally commended if a war is going on. Our antimilitarists, meanwhile, are arrested, charged with maldoings, and punished. Or, as they see it, persecuted.

This case differs from that of the musicians in that the public is more concerned, so that the isolation and glaring become public labeling, name calling, and aggression. It should be remembered, however, that persecution can harden a cult, and in the mutual aggression which follows, we cannot predict at the outset who will win. To be sure, many similar movements perish under suppression, but notable exceptions have drawn wisdom from their tribulations, organized more effectively, become welded together in their hardship, and ultimately reshaped their society. The Nazis were one such movement.[2]

The purposes of a social movement cannot be evaluated, nor the actions of members understood, unless we clearly perceive the background of the society against which they play their part. Social movements, like man's other works, are made of the stuff that is at hand. Their purposes rarely depart entirely from those of their society; some roots are usually to be found. Similarly, their methods must be understood in terms of the experiences of the people within and without the movement. This is sometimes easy, when studying local movements, because we know and feel a great many things about our own society without any special effort. In a heterogeneous society, however, we cannot assume that we understand how others feel, and when we study a movement in some foreign society the problem of obtaining a sound perspective often becomes enormous. For example, the average American would be at a loss to make sense out of the movement led by Mahatma Gandhi in India without a well-directed study of the history and

[2] The circular development of anxiety, conflict, and solidarity is examined in detail by Lewis Coser in *The Functions of Social Conflict*, Glencoe, Illinois: Free Press, 1956.

ways of the Indian people. The technique of *Satya-graha** seems incredible to most Americans, and many solemnly asserted: "It just won't work." But it did. Given enough background we can see how and why it did, and even generalize about the possibilities of similar techniques being effective elsewhere, including our own society.

To understand a movement, it is often desirable to classify its purposes relative to those of the rest of society. Such a classification also provides an initial thumbnail description of the purposes. For this classification four familiar concepts are suggested: *reactionary, conservative, revisionary,* and *revolutionary.*

These words, like many good words in our language, have undergone considerable abuse. They have been used vituperatively by so many people that their original meanings are virtually lost. In this context, they are not intended to praise or to condemn; they are merely meant to relate the position of a social movement to that of the society around it.

We have said that movements draw upon the past. *Reactionary* movements are those advancing aims which were once held by the general society but which have subsequently been laid aside. The members of the movement want to return to some part of the past which to them may be "our grand and glorious heritage," "the solid foundations upon which our nation was builded," or just "the good old days." The point is not whether these purposes actually support the "good old days" or the "bad old days" but simply that society once held this position (or is assumed to have done so), does not now hold it, and that the movement seeks to create it again.

Conservative movements seek to maintain the status quo. This may appear paradoxical, in view of the earlier statement that movements seek to alter or supplant. However, societies and cultures are not static; they keep changing. Thus when we call a movement conservative, we mean that the purposes it holds have for some time

* This was the prototype of "passive resistance."

been those of the society, but change is taking place, and the movement is organized to obstruct this change. Obviously, conservative movements are most likely to spring up when there is a threat of change, and they are frequently organized specifically to combat the activities of some other movement which is making changes. Many conservative movements are thus reactive, or "anti" movements. There is a strongly shaded difference, however, between a movement which reacts conservatively to impending change and a true "reactionary" movement which wants to reestablish something which has already changed.

Revisionary movements accept some of the present purposes and methods of the existing order but wish to modify these—as, for example, the parliamentary socialist movements, and the various movements organized for the "improvement" of this or that. Change is desired, but the existing structure as a whole is not threatened. The distinction between revisionary and revolutionary is a matter of scope or degree, the revisionists working for partial, or slight, changes.

Revolutionary movements reject the existing social structure as inadequate, wishing to supplant it with one considered to be more suitable. This total change has sometimes been called "radical," after the Latin word for root. Revolutionaries want to change the plant from the roots up. It seems better, however, to reserve the term radical to refer to the intensity and not the direction of the actions, because a reactionary may also want a complete change. In other words, one may be radically reactionary or radically revolutionary. Other meanings may be ascribed to all of these words, but these are the ways the writer prefers to use them. Revisionary and revolutionary movements differ in the degree of change which they seek; a revolutionary movement wants to change much, perhaps most, of the existing society.

Still another kind of purpose may be discerned in some social movements—that of *escape*. In this case no direct attempt is made to deal with the present culture at all, but rather the members try to remove themselves from it, either by actual physical isolation (as with Marcus Garvey's "Back to Africa" movement and the Mormons in their exodus to the West) or by developing a kind of sect which may be "in the world but not of it." The degree to which a movement provides escape varies greatly, but certainly it is one characteristic of most cults and nearly every secret society. Hadley Cantril has discussed this aspect of the Kingdom of Father Divine,[3] and pointed up the psychological difficulties involved when isolation seems called for, but is only partially achieved.

One writer distinguishes between "norm-oriented" and "value-oriented" social movements.[4] But while these and other distinctions may prove useful, the test of all concepts is the same: concepts are good if they promote understanding, bad if they impede it, and superfluous if the distinctions they pursue are not found to be related to important consequences in the real world.

Not all movements of course can be catalogued neatly under this system—as exclusively one or another of these types. Nor do all evidence a single, clear-cut purpose. As was pointed out in the discussion of numbers, when people know each other intimately they may discover more than one common desire, and may set up a variety of purposes. Also, as a matter of expediency in obtaining the support of a large number of people, the movement may espouse various purposes, not all of which are logically necessary to each other. When for any reason more than one purpose is involved, these may be related differently to the society. Thus a large movement may be reactionary in some respects, revolutionary in others, and mildly revisionary in still others.

[3] Hadley Cantril, *The Psychology of Social Movements,* New York: John Wiley and Sons, 1941. In paper: Science Edition, 1963.

[4] See Neil S. Smelser, *Theory of Collective Behavior,* London: Routledge and Kegan Paul, 1962.

When these purposes do differ we should examine them separately for even the observation that they differ is often significant. We should also inquire why different purposes are included. Perhaps it exhibits the whims of some strong leader, who has managed to fasten his own irrational valuations on the movement. Perhaps it is hostorical accident, growing out of unreasoned traditional loyalties and hatreds. Perhaps it is a carefully contrived scheme to placate or deceive some powerful group who might oppose one of the purposes if it were taken by itself. Or perhaps it indicates that the movement is not a single body at all but rather a coalition which at present pools its efforts to obtain certain goals, but which may later divide into antagonistic factions.* Understanding why differing purposes are included may help to predict the progress of the movement, its probable successes and failures, and the kinds of opposing social structures which could control or destroy it.

Duration

In inquiring about duration, we imply that, in order to be called a social movement, the behavior we are studying must appear more than once. It must be repeated in some organized fashion if we are to feel justified in linking together observations which we have made on several successive occasions and calling them a social movement. This distinguishes a social movement from some other collective behavior such as panics or riots, lynch mobs, walkouts, and so on, all of which may have a temporary or spontaneous character and frequently are not so much planned as "just happen." Moreover, while they are not so unique that they occur only once, when they do recur they have no necessary continuity, either

* This appears to be the case in two current movements, the Negro civil rights movement (or movements) and that of the expatriot Cubans opposing Castro.

as to plan of action, organizational structure, occasion, or personnel.

Admittedly, the nicety of this distinction exceeds the nicety of reality. In some instances riots, which usually have the temporary character mentioned, have been planned. Some social movements use the riot as a specific tactical weapon for gaining their purposes and employ it repeatedly and systematically. So, too, other movements have deliberately created and controlled panics, walkouts, and lynchings. In other words, although these explosive and fragmentary occurrences are not in themselves social movements, typically lacking consistent duration and planned organization, they may be a part of the activity of a social movement. This being so, they will be classified and discussed later along with other methods employed by movements in instrumenting social action.

The questions regarding duration are simple and to the point: How long has the movement been in existence? Has there been an unbroken line of activity, or has the movement flourished and withered sporadically? Are there distinct periods or phases of its past history? What is its apparent life expectancy today?

In citing duration as a characteristic of a social movement, we should not be led into the trap of denying recurrence or independent invention. History records many ideas or techniques which have appeared, flourished, and then disappeared, only to spring up again later in the same or similar form. Likewise, if we assume that social movements come into being for necessary and sufficient causes (even though we may be unable to describe these exactly), it is apparent that the same or similar causes may operate to produce a similar social movement in several places at once, without close communication between the various groups. In the 1920's in various parts of Germany, movements sprang up which were not directly related to each other, but which apparently were similar independent responses to a number of generally felt social conditions.[5] Later, as often happens, most of these become absorbed into several large organizations through coalitions, but such an amalgamation is historical rather than necessary. Essentially similar movements can continue independently and coalitions may later subdivide. These events characterized the several temperance or anti-alcohol movements in the United States, and the recent burst of civil rights agitation by Negroes and their sympathizers.

In discussing duration, we must also distinguish what it is that endures. A movement may continue to pursue the same objectives, and with much the same organization and techniques, even though individual members are replaced, as an army unit may trace its history back to its most famous leader, whereas the membership has been totally replaced time and time again. Conversely, there may be a continuity of persons who remain together through successive shifts of policy or purpose and win organization and name. However, if we find neither sort of continuity, it is hardly meaningful to speak of a social movement. The loose usage of the term "mass movements" by some writers to refer to a wave of interest in some fashion or a general unrest or civil disrespect weakens any technical meaning the term "movement" might have, and ignores other vocabulary describing such phenomena. A public is not a movement any more than a crowd is, and meaning is lost by sloppy usage.

There is no characteristic life cycle of social movements. That is to say, the particular historical development of a social movement is determined by so many variables that its success or failure, the speed of its growth or decline, the consistency or inconsistency of its operations will not fit any *a priori* formula. If we quantify the development of a movement by counting mem-

[5] See: Howard Becker, *German Youth: Bond or Free,* New York: Oxford University Press, 1946. Robert G. L. Waite, *Vanguard of Nazism,* Cambridge, Mass.: Harvard University Press, 1952.

bers, amount of income and expenditure, number of outside persons reached, number of pieces of literature, and so on, we find great variation.[6] Other writers have sought, with limited success, for the life cycles of restricted kinds of movements, as, for example, political revolutions.

Some movements grow very slowly, either through choice, as in the case of the Jesuit order, or because the purposes are abhorrent to most of the population, as in the case of nudism in the United States. Others seem blessed with the vitality and reproductiveness of a mushroom and accumulate personnel and property with great rapidity, as the earlier Back to Africa movement among Negroes led by Marcus Garvey, and the recent "Black Muslims." Sometimes the early success of a movement is conditioned by special social circumstances of a temporary nature, so that it skyrockets into prominence and then almost as quickly declines. The depression of the 1930's, for example, gave birth to various social movements. Technocracy, a movement championing a special type of economic reorganization, burst into public prominence in the early days of the depression, and quickly faded, leaving only a few traces, although it is still mildly active in Cleveland, Ohio. The Townsend Plan, another economic movement which grew rapidly during the 1930's, has also declined but has not yet entirely perished.

Usually it is easiest to see the progress of a movement in retrospect, after all the data are in and the movement has ceased to exist. However, because of the publicity value of traditional names and ideas, we can rarely be certain that a movement is totally defunct. The classic example of a movement which has been reborn is the Ku Klux Klan. The Klan has appeared on at least three separate occasions, in a variety of places, and the successive

[6] C. Wendell King, *Social Movements in the United States*, New York: Random House, 1956 presents a discussion of the life history of several social movements and some interesting speculations as to the important determinants of a movement's "career."

rebirths have been marked by differences in purpose, in methods, in personnel, and in general social significance. This could be true of other movements, given the right conditions. New wine may certainly be presented in old bottles. Who can say positively that there will never be a resurgence of the Industrial Workers of the World, or of the Nazi Party? On the surface the first looks unlikely and the second dangerously plausible, but we cannot be sure. The existence and success of a movement are concrete, practical facts. And although it is tautological to say it, we must recognize that a movement succeeds and continues when it offers something that people want, and it ceases to exist when people no longer want what it offers, or when they can get it more satisfactorily by other means.

Using the term "want" at all offends many psychologists, who find it difficult to specify any dependable content to the word. However, since people commonly phrase their own views of their motives in terms of "needs" or "wants" or "desires," it is difficult to avoid using these terms without elaborate and pretentious circumlocution. I would only argue quietly that if a man thinks he wants something, he will try to get it, and if he tries to get it, probably he will insist that he does so because he wants it. This is not to say that whenever something is functional to a social system it will persist. History records many "needs" of societies which long went unmet, as well as the loss of objects or practices essential to other important activities.[7] However we phrase it, some movements fail for lack of a felt need for their wares, others because of more effective competi-

---

[7] A classic early reference is: W. H. R. Rivers, "The Disappearance of Useful Arts," originally published in Festskrift tillegnad Edvard Westermarck i anledning av hans femtioarsdag den 20 november 1912. Helsingfors: J. Simelii arvingars boktryckeri, 1912.
Reprinted in the University of Chicago Syllabus for Social Science I, September 1934, and elsewhere. Rivers shows how bows and arrows, canoes, and pottery all disappeared in cultures where they were demonstrably useful.

tion from rival agencies, and still others by working
themselves out of a job.

In discussing numbers it was said that different methods of control are suitable to different-sized movements.
Similarly, different means of communication and different techniques of other kinds must be employed as a
movement changes in size. Since the history of most successful movements is one of a gradual growth, we may
expect accompanying but not necessarily gradual
changes in other characteristics. As a movement attains
sufficient numbers and influence to become prominent
in the public view, outside influences are brought to
bear, attempting to obstruct the activities of the movement and to pervert them to serve other ends. Opportunists of all sorts begin to climb on the bandwagon.
Professional leaders offer their services and in some
cases replace the founders, who are often amateurs un-
skilled in the kinds of political tactics which may be required to hold their place at the helm.

These changes may occur gradually, and transition
from one leader to another or from one alignment of policy to another may occur without attracting notice.
Very often, however, minor crises occur, in which authority or policy shifts under dramatic circumstances,
and these sudden shifts mark off distinct phases in the
movement's development. For example, a number of
writers have noted this aspect of the famous "beer hall
putsch" of the early Nazis, and in the Mormon exodus.
Frequently the death of a leader marks the end of a
phase or period of development, as may external events
of catastrophic or providential nature. The whole question of leadership is somewhat fuzzy and hard to generalize about, but the phenomenon of the "second leader"
is so widespread in the development of social movements that it deserves special attention. Whether fate,
systematic search, self-selection, or conquest occasions
the replacement of the founder by a successor, important changes in the movement often coincide.

In trying to explain man's complex behavior, people

have often fastened onto various simple formulas. Some hold that man is basically the same as he has always been and that the careful cataloguing of his actions shows what can be expected of him. Others insist that man's nature is constantly changing, that he is never the same twice, and that our only hope of understanding lies in trying to chart the direction of these changes, as a physical scientist might plot the movement of a glacier or an avalanche. Even the notion of *understandable* change is denied by some persons, not all of them pessimists, who hold that capricious and unpredictable outside forces are the real molders of history. And like the Blind Men of Indostan, "all are partly in the right and all are in the wrong."

Evidently, history of any aspect of man's behavior, individual or collective, does not fit perfectly into any of these patterns. Some characteristics do remain the same, at least in some perspectives, for a long period of time. But to insist that constancy is the essence of man challenges all sorts of deviations for which some kind of account must be made. Again, there are clear instances of slow, and predictable change, whether the evolving or maturing of some usage or institution, or merely the wear which use always entails. But to insist on a regular change theory, be it evolution, progress, or entropy, denies salient instances of both constant phenomena and sudden, dramatic deviations from the projected line.

The student of social movements, like any other student of human behavior, will do well to be alert to three kinds of characteristics of his subject. He will probably find constant, unchanging aspects. He will also find measured, gradual changes. And he will from time to time perceive sudden intrusive forces—"accidents," "traumatic experiences," or "acts of God"—which explode unforeseen on the horizon to shatter, redirect, or reenergize the movement he is studying. The general theory of historiography is both absorbing and difficult, and it is unlikely that many sociologists will approach a mastery of it, but since any study of phenomena which are measured in time is in some sense historical, it is a good idea to become acquainted with at least the simplest basic problems of historical study.[8]

Knowledge of phases or changes that have taken place in a movement may help predict its life chances in the future. Thus a movement which has shown a facile and sensitive responsiveness to changing conditions around it, and which has altered its structure, or policies, or personnel so as to keep up with the times, has a better prospect in the face of future demands which general social changes may make upon it than one which has rigidly adhered to obsolescent formulas and senescent leaders, despite failure to attract support.

Related to this is what we might call the "self-insurance" of the movement. A basic principle of insurance is to spread the individual item risk over a large number of items, relying on the statistical chance that not all of them will be lost at any one time, and balancing out the failures against the successes. A business concern whose holdings are sufficiently large and diverse is in a sense self-insured. By analogy, so too is a social movement, not merely in the economic sense, but in other ways as well. This self-insurance is well known to politicians, as political platforms clearly reflect. Enough programs are presented to appeal, at least segmentally, to nearly everyone. Thus if a few programs fail, and some adherents are lost thereby, others may be well satisfied. If this procedure can be carried to the point of demonstrating tangible success with at least one or two policies which are desired by the majority of members, the movement may live and prosper even though some important aims are not attained. While a small, ideologically pure movement must give promise of meeting its limited objectives and support its members' morale rather directly in this way, a larger movement with a "shotgun" program may survive numerous minor setbacks by diverting members'

---

[8] A good, readable book for the student is: Frederick John Teggart, *Theory and Processes of History*, Berkeley: University of California Press, 1960.

attention to other plans and other actions. The questions of what degree of satisfaction the members will require and what measure of hope they will hold in the face of tangible results are ones which can be answered only through a clear understanding of the motives of the members and the patterns of individual behavior which the movement has power to control. If the aims of the adherents can be identified, and the degree of discipline assessed, and the likelihood of the aims being realized through the movement can be determined, prognosis for the movement becomes fairly clear. The term "prognosis" is used advisedly, however, because this operation, like clinical medicine, is more of an art than a science. At best, we can judge how it is going, and not prophesy where it will end.

An Example: The Black Muslims

An interesting current social movement in the United States is The Nation of Islam, also called the "Lost-Found Nation of Islam," and commonly known as the Black Muslims. The variant spelling is intentional, the members having little connection with the eastern Moslems, although they claim such a lineage as proof of their long duration. Probably originating around 1930 as a schism from an earlier movement called the Moors, the Black Muslims were led at first by Wallace D. Fard, of whom little is known, and the movement was brought to prominence in the 1930's by Elijah Mohammed (Robert Poole).

The common background and purpose of the Black Muslims are suggested by Essien-Udom:

White middle-class society, in reality, is not, and for a long time to come may not be, open to the millions of black Americans. But, in fact, neither is Negro middle-class society open to them. The inferior material and cultural standards of the Negro masses prevent them from entering either society. . . . For this reason the Negro masses are instinctively "race men." [9]

In other words, the basic problem of the mass of urban Negroes is that they are lower class and social conditions are such that few can rise on the social ladder. Thus their purpose is almost ready-made: band together and change the restricting social conditions to permit social and economic mobility. Since their problem is unique to Negroes, so too is their appeal. Few whites, even if they could, would join a movement which declares all whites to be the natural enemies of all blacks. Many blacks will join, however, because the Muslims' oversimplified view of the problem absolves them of guilt and past personal responsibility at the same time that it offers the possibility of future reward when their numbers permit them to establish a new social order.

How many members do they have? In 1962 Essien-Udom estimated their strength at about 250,000 in 21 states and the District of Columbia.[10] They center in the large urban areas, where their temples are closely watched by the "white devils" who surround them. Conflicts have been few, because, despite the vehemence of some of their accusations against white society, they have led mild lives. Although they advertise themselves as a revolutionary group, they behave more like another escapist cult. Their reward is supposed to come on earth, and not in heaven, but it is not appreciably more immediate than the Green Pastures of the old gospel preacher. Curiously, however, on the basis of this frankly materialistic appeal a rigorously ascetic life is prescribed, and widely followed, which sharply contrasts with the stereotype of the happy, carefree "Negro on Saturday night."

[9] E. U., Essien-Udom, *Black Nationalism,* Chicago: University of Chicago Press, 1962, pp. 2-3. This book is available in paper as Dell 0574 (Laurel Edition).

[10] Other estimates, of course, vary. See: Eric Lincoln, *The Black Muslims in America,* Boston: Beacon Press, 1961. This appears in paper as BP 137.

As we might expect, people caught in the position of being unable to assert themselves because of their visible differences will be ambivalent about these differences. This has long been true of many Negroes, who have alternately boasted of their racial traditions (usually with an inadequate knowledge of them) and privately cursed them. Similar circumstances should call forth similar movements, and Negro separatist movements have a long history. The most notable early exponent was Marcus Garvey, but there have been others, and the Black Muslims are neither the most recent nor unique, although a current example. If we loosely date this movement back to Garvey, it has been operating since about 1915, with changes in leadership and with various interruptions. If we insist on continuous leadership and overlapping membership, it dates at least from the early 1930's in Detroit, and is a little more recent elsewhere. Its greatest period of growth has been since the Korean War, and there does not appear to be any decline at the present time.

Perfectionist cults, regardless of aim, tend to divide and divide again. The Black Muslims originated in one such division after the death of the leader of an earlier movement. With the physical decline of Elijah Mohammed, several younger leaders sought to emerge. One of the most promising and for a time most successful was Malcolm X (Malcolm Little). The son of a preacher who had followed Marcus Garvey and died violently, Malcolm participated in most of the sordid experiences which are accorded lower class urban Negroes. He made a living in various forms of crime and near-crime and in 1946 was sentenced to 10 years in prison. Like many other Muslims he was converted while in prison and upon his parole in 1952 became active in the cult, becoming one of its foremost spokesmen by the late 1950's. More violent in his speeches than most of the other official speakers, he was finally suspended in 1963 after he made outrageous comments on President Kennedy's assassination. From this time forward he led his own version of black nationalism and threatened to split the movement wide open through his fervent appeals. At a mass rally in Harlem on Sunday, February 21, 1965, he was shot down as he rose to address his followers. His slayers were allegedly executioners from the Black Muslims and threats of reprisal and unrest have rocked the black nationalist movements since. Whether further splits will occur and new leaders will emerge cannot yet be said for certain but the pattern suggests the possibility.

The Muslims demonstrate the characteristics of social movements we have so far described. They have large numbers, long duration, and clearly articulated purposes, ranging from conservative to revolutionary. They espouse a complete domination of the society, but make their members lead circumspect lives, avoiding indulgence in alcohol or tobacco, treating women with great respect, and dressing and speaking with a sober formality which is something of an exaggeration of the Victorian model of the middle-class white.

Yet while the questions of numbers, purpose, and duration are important criteria of social movements, there are still other questions concerning social movements which are fruitful to ask. In the following chapter, for example, we will examine categories of membership, attitudes expressed toward new members, and the place which a social movement occupies in the life of the member. The brief description presented here of the Black Muslims does not go into these questions, but answers to some of them may be found in the cited books by Lincoln and Essien-Udom, as well as in the ample bibliographies which these authors have collected.

Chapter II

MEMBERSHIP

Categories of Membership

Study of any social movement shows that only certain kinds of people join. These "kinds" vary from one movement to another, but some categories recur so frequently that we can save effort by examining them before looking for more unusual or more subtle similarities.

At least two processes operate in the selection of members. First, people of different ages and in different walks of life have different opportunities and encounter different problems; they develop different abilities and techniques; they evolve different attitudes. Consequently, they will appraise the social scene differently and assign different values to the purposes and promises of a social movement. Thus a social movement which appeals strongly to young rural males may seem insignificant or even abhorrent to old urban females.

Secondly, a social movement appeals to a particular category of people not only because of their similar purposes, but also because its membership already includes their kind of people. For example, the writer studied a movement, which at the outset could plausibly have appealed to members of almost any racial or ethnic minority, but which in fact attracted members of only three

minorities, plus a few members of the "white Protestant
majority." Thus while there was no attempt at exclusion
—quite the contrary in fact—the Catholic membership
did not increase as rapidly as the others, and more of
them became inactive. The membership committee easily persuaded other members of the Jewish community
to come, since they could refer to friends who were already members, whereas Catholics did not perceive the
same appeal. The Jewish members of the membership
committee complained that there were too many Jews in
a movement which needed a wider range of people, but
there did not seem to be much anyone could do about
it.

Both to pursue common needs and for congeniality,
social movements tend to attract restricted categories of
members. Let us consider some recurrent categories:

Age. Age alone is not a precise index of abilities, but
it has been accepted as one for so long that it influences
most people's attitudes as strongly as if it were an abso-
lute quality in itself. Certain age categories are thus
handicapped by being defined as "too old" or "not old
enough" for desired roles in their society. Some movements appeal to these disenfranchised persons. In this
respect, the German youth movement[1] is instructive. A
different kind of youth movement is the Boy Scouts.
Among oldsters, the Townsend Plan[2] is an example.

Sex. Most societies discriminate on the basis of sex.
Many social movements attract principally or exclusively one sex. Two "female" social movements are the
Women's Christian Temperance Union and the Suffra-
gettes.

Occupation. Since occupation is closely related to
standard of living in modern societies, some movements
seek to improve the position of one or a few occupa-

---

[1] See Howard Becker, *German Youth: Bond or Free*, New
York: Oxford University Press, 1946.

[2] For a brief summary of the Townsend Plan, see Arnold Green,
Sociology, New York: McGraw-Hill Book Company, 1960, pp.
640 ff.

tions, as in guilds, labor unions, farmers' organizations, and special political parties closely related to occupations.[3]

Economic class. If one were to accept broadly Marxian theory, all social movements should spring from class memberships, and should seek class-oriented purposes. And indeed some movements do appeal especially to one class. As with age, the appeal is most likely to appear in categorical terms when individuals are labelled by their society as belonging to a category and when belonging is a disadvantage. Under conditions which Marx described disadvantaged economic classes do tend to develop social movements in order to change the society to their advantage. Various "poverty armies" have besieged executives and legislatures, and some early labor movements were manned principally by people from the lower economic classes. However, since class lines are unclear in the United States, there are probably no examples of social movements here whose membership could be defined by economic class alone. Yet, in conjunction with other categories, class is often significant. For instance, the League of Women Voters tends to have a middle-class membership, as does the Boy Scouts of America. Most Pentecostal religious movements have a largely lower-class membership and some nationalistic economic-political movements have appealed primarily to the upper class.

The significance of social class membership is complicated. People who are really downtrodden do not often form political movements, or indeed anything, except escape movements. History has rarely recorded a successful slave revolt. Where movements have emerged representing the depressed classes in a society they have often as not been led by people of higher social status, and financial support has often come from outside.

[3] See Thomas H. Greer, *American Social Reform Movements,* New York: Prentice-Hall, 1949; and Carl C. Taylor, *The Farmers' Movement 1620-1920,* New York: American Book Company, 1953.

Even escape cults among down-and-outers are often
borrowed rather than indigenous. It might seem that
surplus energy must be available for people to form or
join a movement to change things. People who are
barely surviving are often neither able to afford the in-
vestment nor the risk of membership in a social movement.

In reviewing similar observations, Lyford P. Edwards
wrote:

The explanation in all these cases is the same: Revolutions
do not occur when the repressed classes are forced down to
the depths of misery. Revolutions occur after the repressed
classes, for a considerable time, have been in the enjoyment
of increasing prosperity. A marked increase of power, intel-
ligence, and wealth in the repressed portion of society is a
phenomenon invariably found in the period preceding any
great revolution. It is one of the most important symptoms
of future upheaval.[4]

Education. If education is effective, it can change the
personality of the educatee. New similarities appear in
similarly educated men with regard to abilities,
attitudes, needs, and the recognition of problems. Consequently, education influences the probability that a
man will join a given social movement. In this regard,
three influences can be profitably distinguished: the
general level of education, special technical education,
and "the old school tie."

A leader must speak to his people in their language;
by misjudging the general level of education in his potential followers, he may frighten them away with
schoolbook grammar, or offend them with value-laden
idioms or grammatical blunders. Just as sufficient factual
and methodical material is retained by people after
graduation so that most high school graduates cannot be
fooled by some statements which would convince fourth

[4] Lyford P. Edwards, *The Natural History of Revolution,* Chicago: University of Chicago Press, 1927, p. 36.

grade graduates, so, too, college graduates may be convinced by some arguments which would not appeal to others. Admittedly, our formal educational process is not wholly effective in changing people, and much education along the same lines that schools offer can take place outside of schools, so that the general level of education is a crudely measured characteristic. It is, however, a real one.

Special technical education is narrower and a better predictor, since it is often closely associated with age, sex, occupation, and income. Thus a movement may appeal strongly to doctors or engineers or ministers, because their technical education has produced similar qualities among them. For example, they probably share a common vocabulary. A considerable number of electronic engineers joined the Dianetics movement, largely because the language of the movement, and the analogies of its reasoning, were culled from electrical engineering, even though the problems the movement attempted to solve are usually handled by psychiatrists.

The "old school tie" influence refers to extracurricular traditions which arouse sentiments among old grads: "The Commons," "The Ivy," "The Fighting Irish," "The West Point Ring," "Senior Walk," "The Whiffenpoofs." Some "traditions" continue for years; others characterize only one college generation: "slickers," "Four Horsemen," "raccoon coats," "goldfish."

Such shared recollections may symbolize all that is young and vital, honorable and true, and since many of us sentimentalize our waning youth, the old school tie can mean more in frayed and spotted middle age than it did when we first wore it. Writers have frequently described the traditional obligations of loyalty of West Pointers, Cambridge graduates, and others. Among Germans the duelling scar, earned in a carefully contrived but potentially dangerous duel between college fraternity men, was long a symbol certifying that the bearer came from a good family, had been reared to respect honor, and had proven himself a man worthy of respect in return. In the United States its counterpart has often been the football cleat mark.

Along with this nostalgia goes the overevaluation of the intellectual abilities and judgments of one's fellow alumni displayed by many graduates of any school having serious pretenses to an intellectual tradition, and some which do not. The Oxford Group, the Fellowship of Reconciliation, and the Fellowship of Christian Athletes have appealed to "old school tie" sentiments. Some of the recent liberal groups whose propaganda output is keynoted by signed full page advertisements in metropolitan newspapers have assimilated this device by making it clear that contributors' names will be listed with those of prominent alumni whom they presumably respect. The snobbery involved varies from gross to subtle, and the approach is widely and successfully used.

Racial or ethnic background. Nearly every identifiable national, racial, or ethnic category has been "represented" by a social movement. Examples include the Bundesbrüder, Sinn Fein, Mafia,* German American Bund, N.A.A.C.P., The Triad, United Slavonians, Ancient Order of Hibernians, The Imro, Black Muslims, and many others.

Religion. Numerous social movements promulgate some minority religion; others spring from religious contexts to extend over other areas of life. Examples include The Kingdom of Father Divine, The Church of the Latter Day Saints (Mormons), The Jehovah's Witnesses, The Society of Jesus (Jesuits), The Oxford Group, The Zionists, The Ghost Dance, and Bahai.

Political faith. Political faith should be distinguished from "party" as we think of parties in the United States. In other countries many political parties are the extension of social movements in which some restricted political faith is espoused, whereas our two major parties,

---

* The Mafia began as a political movement; later became a parallel government; is known today in the United States largely as the "syndicate" of crime.

sometimes called "patronage parties," do not so much represent a faith as a convenient organization of various interests which require mutual support. Smaller political parties, such as the old People's Party, the Socialist Labor Party, and the Temperance Party are social movements.[5]

Geographic location. Social movements are sometimes restricted to specific geographic areas, and the geographic connection may be one of several kinds. First, geographic areas may coincide with political divisions, so that the hill people are in a different political unit from the plains people, or the people on one side of a river are in a different country from the people on the other side. Added to this is the fact that geographic structures may facilitate or impede communication so that some people meet and others do not. As the way of life practiced in a given geographic area becomes traditional, sentiments supporting these traditions attach to the area as well as to the activity so that the place and the actions together often become sacred. Those who are from our hills and live as we do are treated much as co-religionists, whereas outlanders are regarded as heathen, apostates, or atheists.[6]

Language. Another factor which may unify people in a social movement is language; not merely the common national tongue but also the sectional, occupational, or class accents, idioms, and jargons. Just as Dianetics appealed to radio engineers, so other movements have appealed to farmers, businessmen, sailors, and housewives, in part because "they speak our language." (Some terms recur in different settings with surprising vigor. The beatnik term "fink" seems to trace to the Industrial Workers of the World, among whom it was a mispro-

[5] Rudolph Heberle is especially concerned with this aspect of social movements. See his *Social Movements,* New York: Appleton, Century, Crofts, 1951.

[6] See Rudolph Heberle, *op. cit.,* Part IV. See also Emile Durkheim, *Elementary Forms of Religious Life,* London: George Allen and Unwin, 1915. In this classic work Durkheim explains the origin of sacred places from the activities associated with them.

nunciation of "Pink," for the hated Pinkerton detectives
who insisted that they should pay for train rides!)[7]

Historical accidents. Historical accidents often serve
to unite people who, having undergone a similar and
important experience, think they share something which
others cannot quite understand. War veterans feel a
sympathy even though they may have served half the
globe apart. Of course, the bond is tighter the more similar the service. "What branch were you in?" "Remember
Bandar Shapur?" "Ever fly with Colonel So-and-so?"
Similarly, the bond is tighter among enlisted men than
between enlisted men and officers.

For many people the historical accident does not even
have to have happened to themselves—a great-grandfa-
ther or two will do, if they came over on the Mayflower,
or sired a Daughter of the American Revolution, although the members might not approve of some of these
ancestors were they around today.

Rudolph Heberle, in his book *Social Movements*, de-
votes a chapter to "Political Generations," in which he
notes that peculiar points of view characterize people
who have grown up at a certain time, unlike those of
people who grew up a little earlier or later. His examples include the American and French Revolutions, the
Civil War and Reconstruction periods in the South, the
Nazi movement, and Russian Communists and anti-
Communist groups.

In addition to the obvious connections between certain categories of people and certain social movements,
there are also tangential connections—to wit, "fellow
travelers" and "interlocking directorates." To discern
why a certain category of people appear in a movement
—for example, why Bop musicians become Moham-

---

[7] See: S. H. Holbrook, "Wobbly Talk," *American Mercury*,
VII, 25, January 1926, pp. 62-65. The I.W.W. began around
1905, declined after 1920, and was barely active in 1949. Holbrook dates the term "fink" back to the Homestead strikes of
1892. As with all folk etymology, there may be competing accounts elsewhere.

medans—one must often look for the "fellow traveler" relationship, in which membership in one movement predisposes people to join another. Such a relationship might be found, for example, between such different movements as vegetarianism, nudism, and temperance, the common theme being that of physical culture or purity of the body. People who join one social movement are, in short, good candidates for others. In fact several writers argue that there is something different about "joiners." Eric Hoffer in *The True Believer*[8] writes that a fanatic without a cause is a lost man, and must hitch a ride on the next passing movement, almost without regard for its actual content. This appraisal may be a little extreme, but some people do approximate his description, as can be seen in the "career patterns" of many members. Apparently, some people just like to join groups, for action and congeniality. Others have self-conscious and clear-cut aims, and selectively join only groups which promise to promote these. Others go through phases which present, on a milder scale, the kind of mobile searching which Hoffer ascribes to fanatics.

In a few cases, membership in a succession of movements may reflect changes in personality organization. Reverend Gerald L. K. Smith's highly public career in right-wing groups might be seen as forming such a pattern. Starting as a rather conservative Protestant clergyman holding a regular pulpit, he then diverged farther and farther toward totalitarian political organizations. Some people who begin as mild liberals move steadily left, a change that often embarrasses a man's friends as their image of him becomes outdated. Such changes can also embarrass a whole party or nation, as in the case of Castro's Cuban revolution. Frightened conservatives viewed this as "communistic" from the start, but many people (apparently including our information agencies) thought it was a socialistic movement, hardly the arm of

[8] Eric Hoffer, *The True Believer,* New York: New American Library (Mentor MP 434), 1958.

Moscow. Whether change did occur, by the time the Russians were emplanting rockets conservatives felt confirmed in what they had long suspected: that liberals and neutrals are naive and the information agencies incompetent and perhaps even corrupt. However, convincing as the events may be to one who held this view from the start, they leave room for argument among others. This may be one of those historic episodes in which a cautious man is disadvantaged all the time, whereas one who adopts a simple categorical view has a fifty-fifty chance of being right!

When movements are oriented toward power or serve as pressure groups, one may expect interlocking directorates; that is, in several movements approximately the same people will hold the controlling positions. This simple key will sometimes trace the continuity of a movement which appears and disappears sporadically under various names and at various places. Indeed, the study of some movements becomes almost the biography of an individual or a small group. For example, some people who have been prominently associated with several social movements (although not necessarily with each other) include Dudley Pelley, Allen Zoll, Merwin K. Hart, William Z. Foster, Eugene Debs, and Linus Pauling. The reader will quickly discover that the movements each has been connected with share a general ideology, some to the right and others to the left of the American center.

Attitudes Toward New Members

Just as different people respond differently to a movement, so also a movement may react differently to them. We may distinguish four policies which are operative in regard to recruiting new members: exclusive, receptive, proselytizing, and coercive.

An *exclusive* movement recognizes that outsiders want to join, but restricts admissions. This is true of

most secret societies. Admissions may rest on tests of
loyalty, personal character, service to the movement,
and so on. Usually, few people are admitted in proportion to those who might wish to be.

A *receptive* movement neither seeks nor avoids new
members; it merely permits them to join if they desire to
do so. This was once the policy of the Ku Klux Klan.
Only if a man expressed a desire to join and some Klans-
man overheard him, would he be invited to attend a
meeting and be accepted.

A *proselytizing* movement sends out missionaries to
gather new members. The insistence and perseverance
with which missionaries plead for new followers often
annoys the public more than the central activities of the
movement. Such movements are trying to change *someone else's* culture, and not just their own.

In attempting to make other people live as they do,
whether they succeed or fail, proselytizers often produce
unrest, since their efforts clearly imply that other's ways
of living are inefficient if not morally wrong. A man may
interpret your attempts to convert him as flattery, or he
may be grossly insulted, depending upon how well he is
impressed with your ways.

Many people are willing to let live all kinds of per-
verse individuals and groups, so long as they are not
bothered, but they seriously object to being button-
holed. However, unless the agents of a movement are
willing to take the chance of alienating neutrals, and of
being rebuffed by more active objectors, most social
movements will not grow.

In the extreme effort to obtain members, a movement
may become *coercive*. When this occurs, it is usually because a show of unanimity is necessary in order to obtain results, as when a union or other organization
claims to represent some whole category of people. If
those who are identified in that category do not belong
to the movement, obviously it does not represent them
and it loses prestige. But if every worker is at least nominally in the union, the union can claim to speak with

the voice of all. Coercion may also occur when the "movement" is actually a device for control of the members, as has happened in totalitarian countries. If a large number of the young people are in the youth movement, the leaders of the country know where to lay hands on them and control is more certain. In short, coercion typically occurs in cases in which, either for external or internal purposes, an appearance of unanimity is required.

A movement may also discriminate with regard to different categories. For example, it may be exclusive of Negroes, receptive toward Catholics, proselytizing toward white Protestants, and coercive toward the small businessmen in the neighborhood.

In nearly every society transitions from one social status to another are marked by ceremonies. These "rites of passage" serve several functions. Sometimes they are tests, which actually determine who is capable and who is not. Sometimes the apparent tests are not decisive but demonstrate competence by candidates who are already accepted. Some writers suggest that severe or punitive ceremonies recompense the old members for the loss of status they incur in lowering the barriers to a new member. Fraternity pledges and Ph.D. candidates are apt to concur in this hypothesis.

Some initiation rituals include a public announcement of the change of status of the individual, so that he will hereafter be treated as a member in good standing, "with all the rights and privileges appertaining thereto." The ceremony may also provide advertising, or social control, by displaying to others the solemn accomplishment of the neophyte. University commencement ceremonies apparently aim at something like this. And, of course, as anyone knows who ever organized a boys' club, initiations are fun.

In some cases, there is a hierarchical structure of membership, marked off in "degrees" as in the Masonic lodge, so that repeated tests and demonstrations are required, and suitably celebrated in ceremonies to demark the individual's progress in the order. This is likely to be the case in mystical movements, and serves well as a control device. Just as the young child is controlled by being told, "You're too young. Wait until you are a little older," so the junior member is told, "You are not sufficiently experienced to judge these things. Wait until you are a member of the Most Judicial High Inner Council." In the child, such talk produces frustration and a determination to grow up. From the junior member it may elicit the fees for further instruction, and more consecrated service. In both cases, however, it protects the authority figure and avoids embarrassing questions. Where the degrees actually indicate levels of ability, the careful maintenance of standards for different levels makes for stability in the organization. Max Weber explores this situation keenly in his discussion of bureaucratic structure and control.[9]

A great deal can be learned about the structure of an organization by examining the kinds of tests and trials imposed, and the kinds of qualifications required. In many cases, where a formal "official" statement of qualifications exists, a little careful research will disclose informal qualifications which often are actually more important. This is true of course of all kinds of hierarchical organizations, and not restricted to social movements.

In some movements the bases of advancement are so distinct that clear and predictable patterns or lines of mobility may be described. The people who "get places" are of certain types, come up through certain jobs in certain branches of the movement, and so on. Mobility may be obtained by payment of fees or by rendering specified services. This adds to the treasury, gets necessary jobs done, and insures practical experience "in the field" for all who may later command.

Hierarchies order both duties and privileges. Someone does the work, and someone gets the reward. The two need not coincide. In a movement dominated by a per-

[9] See A. M. Henderson and Talcott Parsons: *Max Weber: The Theory of Social and Economic Organization,* New York: Oxford Press, 1947.

sonal leader, his friendship may be the key. Sometimes, in movements which put their members in actual danger, there may develop an elite guard, which is the special pet of the leader, and which does the exciting and glamorous part of the fighting, leaving the dogged slugging up to less favored and more expendable troops. If this is recognized generally by the members, their dissatisfaction with such a situation may become the basis for a later defection, a "palace revolution," within the movement. A palace revolution means that an organized corps of members near the top of the hierarchy takes over the organization and replaces leaders.

When Hitler was first developing the Nazi movement, the brown shirted S. A. (Sturmabteilungen) were his favorites, composing his shock troops and bodyguard. After power was consolidated and they became a threat to his own power, because of their love of fighting, his favor was transferred to the S. S. (Schutzstaffeln). The S. A. had shirts, but the S. S. wore tailored uniforms. They were supposed to be at least 6′ 3″ tall, preferably blond and blue eyed, with provable ancestry back to the days of Ferdinand the Great. On June 30, 1934, "The Night of the Long Knives," the power struggle between the two groups was resolved after which the S. S. became the elite guard. Still later there was a struggle between the S. S. and the regular army. In the latter days of World War II, the S. S. deteriorated into just another mixed up military unit, manned heavily by draftees who could never have passed the original physical examinations, and most of whom had not the slightest pride in their association, as is generally true of draftees in any army.

Since palace revolutions are always possible where special favored cadres exist within the larger organization, the skillful leader keeps his ear attuned for murmurs of discontent about the differences in status within the movement, and tries either to conceal these differences or else to explain them to the rank and file as legitimate and necessary to the proper functioning of the organization.

The decision whether to dramatize or conceal status differences within a movement should reflect the prevailing norms of the people. Stalin disdained elaborate uniforms and medals, and probably wisely so, since he claimed to be a proletarian leader. Hermann Goering, as a military hero, reveled in them. If Father Divine or some other "divine" leader rides in a Cadillac or Rolls, who can object? Who would ask God to elbow his way through a subway?

The Place of the Movement in the Life of the Member

Evaluating the importance and function of the social movement in the life of the member raises a series of questions. How much of the member's life is involved in the movement? How is his activity in the movement related to his "secular" activities outside it? If the movement commands most of his waking hours, then its norms could be said to control his behavior, simply because they are the only ones he encounters, and great sacrifices can be demanded from him and obtained. But if his activities are restricted to the second Thursday night of each month (except when this interferes with the bridge club), so many other interests compete for his time, money, and respect that the movement cannot get much support, or even risk asking for much for fear of losing him completely.

Hadley Cantril records conflicts in the minds of the members of Father Divine's movement which stemmed from his insistence that they think only of him.[10] This edict could be observed briefly at meetings, but butlers and cooks had a hard time planning meals and attend-

[10] See Hadley Cantril, *The Psychology of Social Movements,* New York: John Wiley and Sons, Inc., 1941, pp. 135 ff.

ing to other details of their jobs while concentrating on
Father. This kind of problem is faced by any movement
which requires a special way of life for members who
must live in the workaday world. If too great an insistence on single purpose and guiding principle is made
the members simply cannot live up to it without jeop-
ardizing their position in the world. The resulting conflict may be resolved by giving up the movement as "just
too tough." On the other hand, if the bars are set so low
that a man can be a good churchman and a good sinner
too, the prestige of the movement and its claims to
moral superiority will be discredited. The compromise
between Sunday Christians or Sabbath Jews and week-
day businessmen states the same problem in religious
terms, and many religious movements have suffered
splits and schisms over the lines drawn between devout
ethical behavior and backsliding opportunism. In a
modern urban business world few people come close to
living up to the religious principles they proclaim, and
many a preacher has had to choose between softening
his sermons and losing his church. The same problem is
seen in the Communist movements, which can require
disciplined performance of full members, but must tolerate halfhearted effort by fellow travelers.

A man may join a movement initially for at least four
different reasons. He may recognize that the movement
fosters his interests. His recognition is essential—there
may be a dozen movements that serve his interests but if
he does not recognize the interest, or the service, he is
unlikely to join. At times, his recognition may be
clouded by ignorance or propaganda so that he thinks a
movement is working in his interest when it is not. Communism again provides a pertinent example. Although
Communists presumably supported laboring men, in the
United States the Party had less appeal to them than to
some more skilled trades. Communists derided working
men who refused to join as having "false class consciousness" but this did not alter the fact that our laboring
men generally saw no answer to their problems in Com-

munism and did not join. They did join unions, because they thought unions served their interests. But other workers, especially in the white collar fields, have often felt that unions are beneath their dignity and avoid them. Many college teachers who enthusiastically join organizations supporting political candidates, or the United Nations, or civil rights would shun joining a union.

Some people may join a movement that provides congeniality and fellowship, even though it does not foster their interests, or even works against them. This situation comes about because there is often a vast difference between the grand strategy of the movement as conceived by its leaders and the day-to-day activities of its local groups. For example, many World War II veterans joined veterans' organizations, not because they compared the competing platforms and subscribed to the political philosophy of one of them, but rather because a bunch of good guys asked them to drop over to the club for a beer and a game of pool. To many a veteran, the fact that an old buddy was a member of the Veterans of Foreign Wars, the American Veterans Committee, or the American Legion, seemed reason enough for joining.

The relationship between the planned formal structure and the informal structure which develops among the members varies. If congeniality is the chief attractiveness of the movement, the informal relationships may take over, so that the top leaders really have much less command than they suppose. For this reason some movements deliberately stage periodic conflicts over basic issues in order to sort out these members who are with them in principle from those who just came along for the ride.

Sometimes the kinds of local policies which develop differ so much from the national policies that the serious member becomes confused and does not know whether he should be in the movement or not. Such has been the case, for example, in some labor unions in which the top leaders proposed radical changes in the industry, while the locals concentrated on clean washrooms, better drinking fountains, and longer lunch hours. Many a man has entered a union on the basis of the local program only to find that the union nationally stood for things he did not want. The same has been true of farmers' movements, the musicians' union, and of others which appeal to a select category of people.

A third, and very frequent, reason for joining a movement is to attempt to raise one's status by becoming identified with the movement. The great popularity of the burial societies among southern Negroes early in this century attests to this point. The Negro, bottom man on the southern totem pole, had very little in the way of prestige symbols with which to bolster his morale. The burial society provided a partial answer. For a small sum of money he joined a group which promised to give him a respectable public funeral when he died. "When I die I want you to dress me in straight-laced shoes, box-backed coat and Stetson hat." [11] A man aspired to decency in burial, even if he were unable to attain it in life. But to achieve this, funds had to be stretched as far as possible. Other members of the society agreed to march in the funeral parade, resplendent in whatever uniform or ceremonial garb they could afford. Thus both in life, marching behind some deceased brother, and in death, as the principal figure in the funeral, a man could be part of something impressive. Ironically, semantic confusions appeared, and many people who were superstitiously afraid of life insurance and feared that buying it tempted God to snatch them away were perfectly content to join the burial societies, which really offered burial and prestige insurance combined.

Prestige-bearing movements attract people in many walks of life. The old political adage, "If you can't beat 'em, join 'em," is adhered to both in its power implications and for prestige alone. If word gets around that a movement is a bit choosy about its members, and prom-

[11] Copyright 1929 Gotham Music Service, Inc., renewed 1957. Used by permission.

inent names appear on the letterhead, social climbers may try to join. Movements often extensively advertise the prominent people they can wangle into joining, and anyone who is well known in the community is besieged by groups who plead: "We won't ask you for money, and you won't have to take any responsibility, or even come to meetings if you don't want to, but just let us use your name." With one big name, they may get ten prestige-hunters, all of whom will pay dues and one or two of whom may actually do some hard work. Furthermore, in the wake of recent witch hunts, many people hesitantly scrutinize the membership list before joining, judging the organization as respectable and safe from congressional or other investigation only if there are a few names on the list that are beyond reproach. Both "offensively" and "defensively," prestige names are valuable enticements to offer the prospective member.

Other reasons for joining a movement often lie in its use as a personal instrument, a tool to facilitate some personal program, or as a springboard from which to leap to a more valued position in the community. A businessman may affiliate with a movement, seeking new customers. A minister may regard his membership as an extension of pastoral duties. Various people may join mainly in order to open social doors.

A professional politician may join some movements to obtain their voting support. Since most social movements are rather easily joined, and since the willing volunteer usually gets responsible positions, he may plan to establish a record of successful leadership as a basis for running for office.

In extreme cases, people may join a social movement with the specific, but unannounced, intention of "taking over" and perverting it to serve entirely different purposes.* This has been a stock approach of the Commu-

---

* Howard Becker used the term perversion to describe the infiltration, take-over, and subsequent redirection of the indigenous German Youth Movements by the Nazi Party under Adolph Hitler. No sexual aberration is implied, the etymology being straight

nists in regard to all accessible liberal groups. The device is double-edged, because with either of the two most probable outcomes, the Communists win. They despise and fear liberal groups because revolution is unlikely while present conditions are tolerable, and liberal groups produce minor changes which ease unrest. Consequently, liberals postpone or prevent the rise of mass resentment which the Communists hope to engineer into a revolution. In short, the Communists must destroy liberal groups, or subvert them to their own tactical purposes.

The subversion itself is ingenuous. By entering the group, and working hard for its immediate objectives, the Communists seek to establish themselves in positions of responsibility. Then, by careful manipulation of the parliamentary machinery, they try to put through policies congenial to the current "line." This often produces a fight, especially if the original group members realize they have been tricked. In the course of the fight, the Communists may split the movement, and take some followers with them. The split lowers the prestige of the movement, so that if they cannot control it and use its name, they are better off to defile it. The original liberals, meanwhile, have lost whatever public respect they once had. After the actions of the movement under Communist control, and the unseemly fight, they are regarded by the public either as fellow travelers or dupes for having let the Communists in in the first place. No movement is entirely fool-proof against this kind of attack.[12]

The technique of subversion as it is practiced by Communists has been detailed and documented by Philip

---

from the Latin, meaning to turn something away from its original direction.

[12] Most social movements seem schism-prone anyway. Observers who took it for granted that Malcolm X would inherit the Black Muslims from Elijah Mohammed were embarrassed to see him pull out to operate his own movement. See: Louis E. Lomax, *When the Word is Given,* New York: The New American Library, Signet P 2429, 1963.

Selznick in *The Organizational Weapon*.[13] And as he points out, the tactics which they employ have been used against them. The effectiveness of the tactic of perversion lies in its economy and in the access it permits. The perverting forces do not have to organize a large movement themselves; they simply find one which someone else has made and then take control. Not only does this tactic save time and effort, but the infiltrators stand to lose very little if the movement collapses in the process, having done none of the hard work of building it up. Also, the perverters are often known to responsible people and groups and could not influence them directly, but if they can operate through a movement which has previously shown no taint of their ideologies, then, at least for a time, they may have the ear of the authorities and of the public. After a sufficient number of groups have succumbed to their attack, of course, any movement may be suspect, but in the broad strategy of world communism this is but a step.

The question of why people join movements may also be given psychological answers, for example, in terms of W. I. Thomas' Four Wishes: the wishes for security, for response, for recognition, and for new experience. The Townsend Plan was aimed very directly at providing financial security for the aged. Occult societies promise various new experiences. Membership in an exclusive movement whose roster is dotted with famous names promises public recognition of the member's importance.

Similarly, we can ask what the member gains from the persons he associates with in the movement. As we observed earlier, some people join a movement because of the abstract plans and policies; others because they like the people in the movement. How does the group, aside from its plans or its ideologies, satisfy the basic needs of the individual? Tamotsu Shibutani thinks that the "hard-

[13] Philip Selznick, *The Organizational Weapon: A Study of Bolshevik Strategy and Tactics* (The Rand Series), New York: McGraw-Hill Book Company, Inc., 1952.

core" members in social movements fight to gain recognition as part of a successful movement in place of personal esteem which they think they lack. In other words, people with low self-esteem seek power. This hypothesis assumes that one can make up with one "wish" what he lacks in another.[14] Thus while the Townsend Plan promised financial security, it also provided pitch-in suppers and bridge parties. Likewise, although the occult society advertises new intellectual experiences, it usually also fosters emotional response between members. Both personal and impersonal aspects of the movement should be considered in relation to the needs of the individual: either alone may attract members, and both combined are powerful.

Since most social movements do not take up all of a member's time or provide a complete world for him to live in, we must consider the effects of membership on his outside activities. How does membership affect his mobility outside the movement? Is he more or less acceptable to various individuals and groups in the general society because of his membership? The answers will describe a complex relationship between various groups and strata in our society, and will vary from one movement to the next, and vary considerably with time and space. For example, nudism has never been a very popular movement in the United States, although there are official groups of nudists in more than half the states. Membership in the nudist movement, however, probably does not greatly enhance mobility in any part of our society, although many people regard it as harmless. In some areas, occupations, and classes, it is severely disapproved of and members are virtually deprived of the rights which ordinary citizens maintain. Several years ago a college professor was dismissed, apparently because he was an admitted nudist. Most college professors seem to feel that this was not a case for the American Association of University Professors to defend, al-

[14] See: Tamotsu Shibutani, *Society and Personality*, Engelwood Cliffs, N.J., Prentice-Hall, 1961, pp. 447-453.

though a man dismissed because he had supported Henry Wallace found considerable sympathy. In short, nudism decreases academic mobility.

The shifting tides of history make membership in many movements a potential handicap in the future. Had George Washington's armies been unsuccessful, there would not likely be any Daughters of the American Revolution. And even though our independence was achieved, and thereby the descendants of the revolutionists given prestige, membership in the D.A.R. does not automatically confer mobility. In the eyes of some, membership in this group is viewed as an accolade, but others regard it as proof of reaction.

In brief, membership in a social movement differentiates an individual from the mass of society. Difference may be valued or disvalued, depending upon the point of view. As a result, mobility will usually be gained in some directions, and lost in others. However, because suspicions are readily aroused by any noticeable difference, it is likely that more people will react negatively than otherwise to the members of most social movements. Thus if a man is concerned about the reactions of everyone he meets, he is well advised to stay out of movements. Conversely, if he derives his satisfaction from the response of a few, then joining a carefully selected group of movements may facilitate that response.

In describing various categories of membership it was pointed out that a movement may specify different categories for different roles in the movement. It may actively seek some kinds of people, tolerate others, and reject still others. Also noted was the use of some prestige figures for name only. If the movement includes a great variety of people, and especially if these are drawn from segments of the population which are normally aloof from each other or actively antagonistic, two hypotheses should be tested. First, the movement may deal with an issue so fundamental to the interests of all that it cuts across ordinary social lines. For example, if a labor movement in an area known for race prejudice includes both white and Negro workers, possibly the issues are so fundamental to the existence of any kind of workers that members will overlook race differences.

The other hypothesis, especially plausible when the leaders and followers are drawn from different groups, is that somebody is being "used." That is to say, one of the groups has succeeded in selling the other on joining forces because they are needed to supply numbers, money, prestige, or technical skills, but exploitation is actually taking place: only one group stands to profit greatly from the venture.

It is not necessarily the leaders who are always guilty of exploiting the followers. To be sure, the leader may preach a gospel flattering the common man while living luxuriously from the collection proceeds taken from those common men for support of the movement. This has been done so often that most leaders of people's movements are automatically suspect by the press and by their opponents of such deception. But there have also been sincere and hardworking leaders who gave their own money and property to a movement which was milked dry by followers who followed only as long as the money flowed in.[15] Sometimes coalitions form in which each category seeks to exploit the other, although such movements usually fall apart quickly. Subversion and subvention can, in effect, be carried on in nearly any movement and, any movement should be examined with these possibilities in mind. In simplest terms, one must always ask who in the movement is giving more than he is getting, and who is getting more than he is giving? This is a simple enough question, but important and often difficult to answer.

[15] See biographies of Robert Owen, and the history of New Harmony, Indiana.

Why Members Come and Go
An Example: The Sometime Communists

Inquiring why people join, fail to join, or leave a social movement leads to broader investigation of the nature and meaning of the movement itself. *A priori* reasons may be refuted by concrete data. Our "rational" explanations (from an outsider's view) may apply for only a small part of the membership, and different motivations operate for others. This is especially true for large movements like Communism.

People who write about Communists and ex-Communists usually write about those they have known, and sometimes display unjustified confidence in the representativeness of their sample. Such is often the case even when the writer has had fairly direct experiences. And when he has not in fact known any Communists, he may draw some queer caricatures.[16]

Certainly a wide range of people have been attracted to this sprawling and complex social movement. Some were attracted for practical reasons. Short-range practical programs of local Communist groups have often coincided with efforts of non-Communists, and still do. When Communists challenged segregation, for example, some Negroes went along with them. When Communists attacked dangerous working conditions in the factory, many mill hands concurred. (Most Negro members remained only briefly, and squabbles over the role of trade unions periodically disenchanted unionists.)

Other people, far removed from professional politics or the production line, have seen in Marxist literature an explanation of economic and political history. Karl Marx was a German scholar who aspired to be a professor,

[16] For an appraisal of American attitudes toward Communists at a crucial period, see Samuel A. Stouffer, *Communism, Conformity, and Civil Liberties,* Gloucester, Mass.: Peter Smith, 1963. This book reports an extensive public opinion survey made in 1954 at the time of the McCarthy-Army hearings.

with all the dignity, diligence, and snobbery that went
with it. He didn't make the grade, and this may partly
explain his revolt. However, he was still a scholar by
trade and at times a good one. Much of his work was te-
dious but it was also unified with the grand oversimplifi-
cation that characterizes most influential ideas. Marx
summed up the world with a principle—that economic
relationships determine the political and social evolution
of society—and many people have adopted his economic theory who never accepted his edicts about political action. Scholars who follow Marx present a sort of
anomaly, which many frightened or embittered people
today refuse to believe can exist: the non-Communist
Marxists.

Even Marx himself once said, *"Je ne suis pas un Marxist!"* Yet ironically, as Communism moved farther away
from his ideas, his name became more and more the
symbol of the movement. Add to this the fact that his
works are laborious reading, and it becomes easy to understand why the man has been damned by people who
have never read him, and who know at best a distortion
of a few of his ideas.

In *Ideology and Utopia,* Karl Mannheim tells us that
there have long been grand ideas created by man to justify his present way of life or to demand a change of
that way of life.[17] Marx, and the Communist movement,
are a link in a long chain of Utopian movements stretch-
ing back at least two centuries.

Edmund Wilson places Marx and Communism in a
long historical perspective of social changes.[18] His is a
sober and thought provoking book, because it shows
how—to borrow Marxian terms—"the seeds of destruction were planted at the beginning of the movement."
Marx, Engels, Lasalle, Bakunin, Trotsky, and Lenin

[17] Karl Mannheim, *Ideology and Utopia,* New York: Harcourt,
Brace & Company, 1936.
[18] Edmund Wilson, *To the Finland Station,* New York: Doubleday Anchor A 6, 1940.

were strong willed men and conflicts within the movement date from its beginning, and center often in Marx
himself, who apparently distrusted anyone who dis-
agreed with him. Communists strove for a "scientific"
theory, but dogmatism often masqueraded as intellectual authority, and set a pedantic intellectual style.

The liaison of Western intellectuals with Russian
Communism in the 1930's is so time-bound that no one
can fully appreciate it who did not experience the 1930's
himself. Many intelligent people temporized with Communism in this period, either as party members or as
fellow travelers. Yet this distinction itself is difficult to
evaluate. Because of our present official hatred of Communists, anyone who can do so will maintain in his
defense, "But I *never* had a card!" to which the prosecu-
tion can always retort, "Membership was a mere formality; you were a Communist." The truth, however, lies on
neither side; there were lukewarm short-time members
and there were avid long-time fellow travelers.

Since Communism simultaneously has lost its hold on
most western intellectuals and has enmeshed world
affairs, there has been a spate of books by former Communists, former fellow travelers, and former "I-told-you-
soers" explaining why Communism was then and is not
now appealing. One of the most readable of these is *The
God that Failed*,[19] in which six well-known writers from
America, England, and the continent discuss their so-
journ with the movement.

Of these six people, however, several never held a
card, and one the Communists themselves enrolled only
reluctantly. Consequently, the book is often charged
with not representing a fair sample; the six are pointed
to as "talking liberals" who were long on words but short
on deeds and who thus may be generally disregarded.
To some extent the charge is true. However, it may be
countered with the story of Bob Darke, a Borough

[19] Richard Crossman, ed., *The God That Failed*, New York:
Bantam Books, A1229, 1954.

Councillor from Hackney and long-time resident of London's East End. For eighteen years, Darke was an active and influential Communist, resigning in 1951.

I was never a Communist intellectual. I put in my party work "on the knocker." That is a proud and bitter phrase used often enough in the Party to describe the comrades who take the fight out into the streets. It is used to strike a difference between men like myself "who would never desert the Party," and the Arthur Koestlers, the Douglas Hydes, the Charlotte Haldanes, who were "always bourgeois at heart and certain to sell out."

Well, maybe I am bourgeois at heart after all. But I fought on the kerbside, at the factory gate, in strike committees, in a militant march from Stepney to Trafalgar Square. I have walked with an ashplant in my hand confident, even hopeful that the police would be forced to break up our demonstration and give the Party its martyrs. But if this sounds a little cynical to you be assured that much of what I fought for as a Communist I fight for still as a Socialist.

It has taken me eighteen years to realize that I have been carrying the wrong banner in the right fight.[20]

Such a man may be more "typical" than the poets, novelists, and playwrights, whose dalliance with Communism was like a bohemian love affair—something to consummate when you are young and discuss when you are older. Or is there perhaps something peculiar to those who *leave* the Party, something that makes them a group apart from those who remain, so that even plumbers and coal miners who leave are still "leavers" and thus an untrustworthy sample? The Party would surely like us to believe this, and it seems plausible that the backsliders from Communism are not necessarily any better examples of Communists than the backsliders from Methodism are of Methodists.

Why people leave the Party seems no more suscep-

[20] Bob Darke, *The Communist Technique in Britain,* London: Penguin Books, 1952, p. 12.

tible of a blanket answer than why they join. In the
United States some people left when the party became
illegal, but others preferred the underground. In the
midst of a depression, many people joined the party
with a cry of pain, anger, and protest against a system in
which something was apparently rotten. The 1930's fea-
tured social novels of brutal super-realism, rubbing salt
in our economic wounds. Russia, meanwhile, was a far
away utopia. Intensely aware of our own difficulties, we
were almost oblivious as to theirs. As the depression
deepened, the need for some people to believe in Russia
was like the Jewish belief in the promised land, or the
Negro slave's belief in heaven. There just *had* to be a
promised land, or a heaven—this couldn't be all there
was to life!

Communist leaders, of course, skillfully nurtured
these dreams with written propaganda and carefully
conducted tours given to a special few. Yet for anyone
who did not need to *believe* in a Russian heaven, there
was plenty of evidence that things were bad there too.
Intermittently, prominent Communists were accused of
"deviationism," vilified, humiliated, deposed, and here
and there killed. The Kulaks, prosperous peasants who
opposed collectivization, were systematically uprooted,
relieved of their families and their farms, and sent off in
slavery to the work camps and the mines of Siberia, in
the name of Bolshevik progress.

Good Communists explained all cruelty by that diabolical thesis of expediency which tempts any man who
desires social action: "the end justifies the means." "To
make an omelette, one has to break eggs."

Means can be justified by ends, however, only if the
ends seem near, worthwhile, and likely to be attained.
The vague hopes crystallized into the "Five Year Plan"
gave the authority of numbers to proposed physical con-
structions and social achievements. Yet when the five
years elapsed, no monoliths had emerged from the
clouds and they were replaced in turn by new five year

plans, three year plans, and the like. This round-robin became what might be called the tactic of concretized postponement.

The alacrity with which "real Communists" had to follow acutely angular changes in the Party line and shrug off internal conflicts and purges disturbed many fellow travelers and some members. At times the party favored labor unions and at others "trade union communist" was a dirty word in the Party. Men who guessed wrong on specific issues or supported the wrong political candidates were summarily ruled out of the Party and their previous service discredited or denied. In contrast to the advertised inter-racial comradeship, various racial, national, and ethnic fights periodically rocked the Party. In areas where the foreign members comprised as much as ninety per cent, such a quarrel could wipe out the local organization. Each leader who was forced out took followers with him. This was hardly the Dictatorship of the Proletariat, and the Withering Away of the State, this was more like the Reign of Terror of the French Revolution, wherein the Revolution was devouring its own.

Such facts make it hard to sort out the stories of people who were in and out of the Party. Of those who had joined in a spirit of generalized protest, most left when they saw that the things they protested, essentially man's inhumanity to man, prevailed in Russia and in the Party itself. Those who had sought a God in Russia saw that God fail. Others, like Darke and a great many trade unionists in various countries, accepted the Communists as allies in small scale fights. The awakening for some of these came when the Communists decided that the unions or the unionists were expendable in some larger struggle. These union men, tougher minded and more disciplined than the individualistic intellectuals, usually defined the problem as a back alley fight and rolled up their sleeves and struck back. Sometimes they overthrew the Communists and saved their unions; sometimes they lost, and were themselves thrown out; and sometimes in the struggle they saw their unions destroyed.

Louis Fischer,[21] one of the "worshippers from afar" in *The God That Failed,* generalizes what he calls the "Kronstadt" reaction of ex-Communists. In this capsule term he refers to the shock and revulsion at "draconic Soviet suppression of the sailor's revolt on the Island of Kronstadt" by Trotsky in February 1921. Strikes and riots were the sacred tool of the worker against bourgeois bosses, but when Soviet workers struck, they were liquidated. Freedom to strike, freedom to speak, freedom to disagree—all perished in Russia.

For other part-time Party members and fellow travelers, the turning point was the Spanish Civil War. Up until this time Communism might still be viewed as a rosy distant dream. Indeed, in some circles it was fashionable to be a Communist—a little like drinking during prohibition. Membership marked you as a sophisticate, a bit cynical toward archaic values, not intimidated by local mores, and a citizen in the coming new world. Some dropped membership during the war in Spain, and others died there. Many young intellectuals died on Spanish soil, believing they were fighting a war for freedom and democracy; others, disillusioned, died simply because they could not avoid it. The Party had cynically sacrificed many of these high-minded young men, whose romantic nature was better suited to dying as martyrs than to the drudgery of day-to-day cell work. Some who survived rejected Communism and fought to expose it, but some returned to it self-consciously and bitterly.

The war in Spain was not "Kronstadt" for every Bolshevik. With sufficient anti-Fascist hatred a man might justify the Spanish struggle as necessary, a moral stand taken to prove that Communists could never live with Fascists, that is, until the Russo-German pact. Hating Germany one week and loving her the next cost other members.

For still others, the old revolutionary utopian zeal of Marx and Engels died in 1940 when Trotsky was murdered in Mexico. However, in a time when some people

[21] Louis Fischer, in *The God That Failed, op. cit.,* pp. 206 ff.

could ignore lynchings in the deep South and gangster warfare in Chicago, and Hitler's atrocities in Europe, others could ignore a minor murder in Mexico. Even the much later Russian suppression of the Hungarian revolution (1956) did not shake all of the faithful. There was, in short, never any over-all Kronstadt.

Another aspect of the joining and leaving of the Communist Party in America was more pervasive and more subtle and thus less easily documented. The decade of the 1920's saw one of the most widespread upheavals in social values that our country has known. For many reasons most of the articles of faith which Americans had previously lived by became suspect. Many liberals and intellectuals lost faith in conventional religion after World War I and some of them saw Communism as a kind of spiritual substitute.[22] However, as the Communist program in this country remained largely negative, attacking Wall Street, racism, and jingoism, those who sought a substitute for the oldtime religion gradually fell away.

A larger appeal came as the result of the dramatic stock market crash and the depression of the 1930's, when many people lost faith in democratic capitalism and thought Communism the rational alternative. Here again, however, Communism did not offer enough of a program to hold the converts it won. Largely contenting itself with parades, minor riots, and literary attacks on the system, Communism lost out when Roosevelt's New Deal showed positive efforts at improving the situation. Thus whereas young people coming of age in 1930 were often attracted to Communism, those coming of age by 1933 adopted instead the New Deal. To be sure there was considerable loss of faith in the New Deal itself by

[22] I observed this among young Protestants during this period and Nathan Glazer makes a similar observation with regard to Jews. See: Nathan Glazer, *The Social Basis of American Communism*, New York: Harcourt, Brace and World, Inc., 1961, p. 168. See also in this same series: Ralph Lord Roy, *Communism and the Churches*, New York: Harcourt, Brace and Company, 1960.

the time of the 1939 recession, and converts again poured in, but before this could be of much use to the Communists we found ourselves engaged in World War II, and this was a large enough event to attract the commitment of young people who felt the need for actively expressing their concern with the affairs of the country and the world. (Some of the veterans of the Abraham Lincoln Brigade of the Spanish Civil War became combat troops in World War II.)

When we thus sketchily review events of three decades it becomes clear that, to use Marx's own terminology, the "logic of history" clearly did not support the Communist movement in the United States. And, as Russell M. Cooper* observes, "there was something about the whole Communist ideology which was so willingly directed by expediency that it did not foster the kind of intellectual integrity and strength of character that allowed its adherents to face adversity in heroic fashion." This is not simply to say that Communists as individuals were cowards, but that the Communist ideology had so many shallow spots that it was difficult for a thinking man to stay with it throughout the rapid social changes of this period.

With our theorizing thus complicated with fact, let us ask again our basic question: Why did people join the Communist movement and why did they leave it? Is it possible that at one time cold logic compelled joining and that at some other time equal logic indicated withdrawal? Or, are both joiners and leavers equally impetuous, and driven by whims?

The answer is this: There was no single time when it was completely plausible to accept Bolshevism, nor some other precise date after which only an idiot could follow it. Varying mixtures of cool appraisal, calculated risk, personal hopes or despairs, and varying information were involved. And just as no single explanation

* This is one of several insights into this period obtained in conversation with Dean Russell M. Cooper, College of Liberal Arts, The University of South Florida.

can possibly suffice for the whole membership, probably few individuals acted for any single reason. In a movement as widespread and complex as modern Communism, people come and go at all times with varying degrees of emotion and insight. How they draw the balance sheet of impelling reasons varies greatly.[23]

It is difficult to arrive at solid figures for membership as the Communists have operated both above and below ground under several names. Theodore Draper in *The Roots of American Communism*, Nathan Glazer in *The Social Basis of American Communism* and David Shannon in *The Decline of American Communism* provide representative figures.[24]

Estimates from their various sources range between 25,000 and 70,000 members in various Communist or near-Communist parties in 1919. Raids and arrests in January 1920 drove the Communists underground and half or more disappeared from the rolls in one month, falling to around 12,000 in 1921 and after bitter internal controversies in 1922 dropping to perhaps 6,000 members, but after intensive recruitment recovering to around 9,000 in 1923. From 7,500 in 1930 membership rose rapidly (but with great turnover) to some 20,000 in 1933, 30,000 in 1935, 55,000 in 1938 and a peak in 1945 which may have been between 65,000 and 85,000 depending on how you count or whose figures you trust. After a classic fight in 1945 Earl Browder left and took with him perhaps 30,000. In 1946 active recruiting and agitation over housing and Negro unemployment brought the figure up around 73,000, but by August 1948 it had dropped to 60,000 and the long steady de-

[23] Gabriel Almond, et. al. *The Appeals of Communism*. Princeton: Princeton University Press, 1954.

[24] Theodore Draper, *The Roots of American Communism*, New York: Viking Press, 1957. Nathan Glazer, *The Social Basis of American Communism*, New York: Harcourt, Brace and World, Inc., 1961. David A. Shannon, *The Decline of American Communism*, New York: Harcourt, Brace and Company, 1959. These are three of an extended series of books called Communism in American Life, under the general editorship of Clinton Rossiter.

cline had set in. F.B.I. estimates in 1955 showed only 22,000 and by 1956 even the New York City May Day demonstration was a shabby and listless affair. The rate of turnover for American Communism was greater than that of nearly any other movement, reflecting remarkably inconsistent leadership and fluctuating world events as well. Shannon[25] estimates that there may be as many as 250,000 persons in the United States who could reasonably be termed ex-Communists. Some of these are just quietly disillusioned and others have become militant anti-Communists. Few movements have appealed so loudly, attracted so many people, lost them so rapidly, and ousted them so vindictively.

Probably few Americans remain attracted to Communism today. Certainly the number of new converts must be very small. Yet Communism moves today in China, Malaysia, India, Africa, and Central and South America. Their "logical reasons" clearly are not ours.

To sum up, the meaning of a social movement in the life of the member can never be determined purely on *a priori* grounds, rationally constructed by outsiders, however intelligent and scholarly they may be. The simplest basic assertion we can trust is that if people affiliate with a movement they must see something in it for themselves. Only a sympathetic and understanding study of the people directly involved can tell us what it is that they see.

[25] David A. Shannon, *The Decline of American Communism*, New York: Harcourt, Brace and Company, 1959, pp. 361-362.

Chapter III

STRUCTURE AND
RATIONALE

Some Bases of Authority and Appeal

Most men not only wish to have their own way but wish to feel justified in doing so. Convincing others that they are justified also helps to insure that they will continue to have their own way. Thus most social movements develop an elaborate "word world" to support their claims to legitimate power. These observations have been succinctly expressed by C. Wright Mills:

> Those in authority attempt to justify their rule over institutions by linking it, as if it were a necessary consequence, with widely believed-in moral symbols, sacred emblems, legal formulae. These central conceptions may refer to a god or gods, the "vote of the majority," "the will of the people," "the aristocracy of talent or wealth," to the "divine right of kings," or the allegedly extraordinary endowment of the ruler himself. Social scientists, following Weber, call such conceptions "legitimations," or sometimes "symbols of justification."

> Various writers have used different terms to refer to them: Mosca's "political formula," Sorel's "ruling myth," Thurman Arnold's "folklore," Weber's "legitimations," Durkheim's "collective representations," Marx's "dominant ideas," Rous-

seau's "general will," Lasswell's "symbols of authority," Mannheim's "ideology," Herbert Spencer's "public sentiments"—all these and others like them testify to the central place of master symbols in social analysis.[1]

Max Weber described three general ways in which the power to make other people obey may appear respectable or legitimate.[2] These are: (1) authority which is imposed and accepted on *rational* grounds, resting on a belief in the legality of the decisions, commands, and regulations; (2) *traditional* authority, which appeals to the "sacred" attitudes toward what has existed in the past; and (3) *charismatic* authority, which denotes the influence of some powerful and awe-inspiring personality. These are what have been called "ideal types," which could exist separately, but in reality are often mixed.

A very old device, related both to traditional and to charismatic authority, is the idea of *divinity*. Many charismatic leaders have convinced their followers that they were divine or at least divinely guided. Traditional leaders have sought by edict what charismatic leaders have accomplished by demonstration. Moreover, a divine leader enjoys maximum prestige, controlling members' behavior by monopolizing their experiences. Linking the movement with the hereafter and the leader with God closes the circle of life and death. A member can't even run away by dying.

Whether or not an appeal to divinity is feasible depends upon the religious precepts of the group. Even a narrow definition of religion includes a wide range of ideas, some mystical and idealistic, others pragmatic and empirical. And even theistic religions vary. Some adopt additional deities or at least saints from time to time,

---

[1] C. Wright Mills, *The Sociological Imagination,* New York: Oxford University Press, 1959, p. 36.

[2] Max Weber, *The Theory of Social and Economic Organization,* translated by A. M. Henderson and Talcott Parsons, New York: Oxford University Press, 1947. See especially pp. 324-385.

while others regard the age of miracles and of saints as past, and disallow contemporary claimants of special virtues. (It has always been hard to recognize a true saint, no matter how important sainthood may be.) It may seem at first glance that an atheistic movement would prohibit the development of "saints," but even this is not altogether so, as the history of Communism shows.

Hero worship resembles idolatry. Both invest the personage of the hero, god, or idol with sacred attributes which may not be tested or questioned. Both promise prestige to the follower for his abject allegiance. Both generate distrust and hatred between believers and infidels. And both create a problem and a solution simultaneously: the problem of justifying a belief in something which cannot be tested and proved before the eyes of nonbelievers, and the solution of rejecting nonbelievers as immoral, unworthy, or mentally underprivileged. The ability to believe what others regard as absurd proves to the believer his superior worthiness.[3]

Much projection inheres in such operations. It may even approach the degree which clinicians define as paranoia. This profound belief, and the resentment of doubt, is another characteristic of members that isolates them from outsiders and convinces outsiders in turn that people in the movement are crazy. For certainly a movement usually does not attempt to make its members objective, but instead devoted. Thus it becomes difficult to be a good member and a good critic at the same time. A deity who can be doubted need not be obeyed, unless earthly sanctions support his commands.

Another idea which provides a basis for the authority of movements is *Natural Law*. As with religion and the notion of God, it would be hard to say when natural law first appeared. Certainly it was a well developed concept among the Greeks and Romans. Essentially it im-

---

[3] For a general discussion of fanatics, see: Eric Hoffer, *The True Believer*, New York: Harper and Brothers, 1951. In paper Mentor MP 434.

plies that there are universal principles by which the world works and that these are more fundamental, hence more respectable, than any laws which man might invent. This is one of those self-explanatory statements which no one is likely to argue much about until he tries to draw a conclusion from it. Then, friends part. For agreement was reached in the first place by a semantic trick. We don't define "natural" but merely assume that it means "what is." We assume that "what is" is "regular." Thus we can claim to stand for a law that is objective, realistic, and God-given, while castigating our opponents as unrealistic and autistic, and, if they try to defend themselves against our accusation, atheistic and immoral as well.

An abstract agreement to defend natural law comes easy, because everyone wants to be on the side of the right. The hitch appears when we try to specify what the regularity of nature "is." Actually this is about what science tries to do, and science doesn't pretend to cope with all of nature. Rousseau and others, annoyed by the shams and pretenses of a complex urban society, gave an ethical edict: "Be natural," which thought was echoed on Broadway to the tune of "Doin' What Comes Natur'lly." [4] But whereas the musical comedy skillfully avoided censorship by not specifying what it is that comes naturally, so that each could read his own inhibited desires into the lyric, Rousseau, less happily, did try to specify.

Natural law is a glow-word which can supplement virtually any position one wants to take. Hobbes can appeal to a conservative natural law; Locke to a revolutionary natural law. For the religionist, natural law can be the will of God, or for the atheist proof that there is no God. Often it is invoked as a substitute for divine will and retribution by people who need extra-human forces but have no tradition of divinity or religion. The semantics become apparent when we try to define nature. If nature is everything that "is," then any thing that

[4] Copyright 1946 Irving Berlin. Reprinted by permission.

is, anything that man thinks of or does, must be natural. Either that, or we mean by natural only that which is familiar and approved, and by unnatural that which is new or different or perhaps man-made. Few of us could defend this latter notion of "nature." Logically dissected, in short, the term loses its force; but few people dissect it—it is too useful and too comforting to risk examining. Thus "natural" and "unnatural" become debased as do orthodoxy and heterodoxy: "Orthodoxy is my doxy and heterodoxy is your doxy." Nevertheless, debased coins sometimes circulate freely, and social movements with programs ranging from nudism to prudism appeal to natural law.

Another pair of concepts was employed by Karl Mannheim in his book, *Ideology and Utopia*.[5] Simplifying his title concepts somewhat, by ideologies we mean conceptions of the world which are influenced strongly by the position the person occupies in society and which justify and support that position; by utopias we mean conceptions which are organized in opposition to the existing conditions and which picture a "brave new world."

We have only to consider the different views of any situation expressed by people who occupy different positions in it to see how position influences opinion. Clashes between managers, stockholders, and workers in a large industrial corporation illustrate the point nicely. The stockholder's chief interest is in income, which should be as large and steady as possible. He deplores any governmental restriction, labor tie-ups, sinking-fund appropriations, or new expenses. The worker is interested in a steady job, with high pay and pleasant work, attention to his physical comforts and safety, and social satisfactions such as recognition of his achievements and advancements in rank and seniority. Resenting the stockholder who sits back and makes money while not working, he fears that his own security and satisfactions

[5] Karl Mannheim, *Ideology and Utopia*, New York: Harcourt, Brace and Company, 1936.

are jeopardized by the stockholder's greed. The manager, meanwhile, wants a smoothly functioning productive system which improves the quality and increases the quantity of the output, competes successfully with other similar concerns, and achieves a national or international reputation, which of course he identifies as his own.

If we limit our attention only to the distribution of the profits we see the different points of view and the way in which each justifies some stand or other. The worker reasons that since it is his work that makes the product, therefore when more money is made he should have more of it. (Perfectly reasonable.) The manager, of course, knows that mere work is not the important thing —the essence of the success lies in organization. Since he organized the work *he* should receive a salary increase. In addition, since he has his eye on a bigger contract next year, most of the profit should be spent in building a newer plant, reworking the present tools, establishing a reserve fund to cover expenses when some delay occurs in collecting outstanding debts, and to support the experimentation in which he will have to engage if he is to beat his competitors. (Sound and commendable.) The stockholders, meanwhile, figure that the only reason they lent the money to the company in the first place was to make money, and the company agreed in the beginning to give them a large share of whatever money was made. Why then should the company now hold back the money which is rightfully theirs to raise wages and salaries and build new buildings and fiddle around with dubious experiments, when it is obvious that the firm is doing well right now? (They have a point too.)

Indeed, everybody has a point, but one point doesn't win the game. The system obviously cannot operate without all three, and to insist that any one point of view is exclusively correct warps the perspective so that practical policies formed from it will not work. Each of these points of view constitutes an ideology. Each man

sees the whole from his own position, and, like ancient
astronomers, he thinks the universe revolves around him.
Nothing is accomplished by accusing any of the three of
being greedy or unscrupulous. They all may be honest,
but they simply think differently.

Ideologies, in brief, are systems of thinking and talking about a situation which are set up on the basis of a
partial view of that situation, and which tend to support
action now being taken. They are not exactly true or
untrue. They are reasoned out and they are reasonable,
if we make certain assumptions (usually hidden) and
omit certain observations. Their function is to provide
an apology, a rationale, or a justification for something
which we intend to do. We need not worry about which
came first, the intent or the reason, because very likely
they emerged together and one will almost certainly appear when we find the other. People in social movements use ideologies to convince themselves and others
who share their position that the stand the movement
takes is the "right" one, so that they can have their own
way and feel righteous too.

In contrast to ideologies, utopias reject the present
system and propose new ones. The term itself comes
from a book by Thomas More which presented a new
pattern for social life. Many such books have appeared:
*Erewhon, City of the Sun, The Republic, Oceana, Lost
Horizon, Walden II.*[6] After a number of utopian social
movements actually founded trial colonies in this country at New Harmony, Indiana, Oneida, New York, and
elsewhere and most of them eventually failed, and after
the Bolsheviks took over in Russia, several writers attacked the whole notion of utopia. Two of the most inci-

[6] Samuel Butler, *Erewhon* and *Erewhon Revisited,* New York:
Modern Library, 1935. Tommaso Campanella, *City of the Sun,*
in Charles M. Andrews, editor, *Famous Utopias,* New York:
Tudor Publishing Company, 1901. Plato, *The Republic,* various
translations. John Toland, *The Oceana of James Harrington,*
Dublin: J. Smith and W. Bruce, 1737. James Hilton, *Lost Hori-
zon,* New York: Grosset and Dunlap, 1936. Burrhus Frederic
Skinner, *Walden II,* New York: Macmillan Company, 1948.

sive satires are Aldous Huxley's *Brave New World* and George Orwell's *1984*.[7]

Whether people actually can live under idyllic conditions they think they desire has often been questioned. An early sociology text is worth quoting in this regard:

You may perhaps recall Professor James's astonishing picture of his visit to a Chautauqua. Here he found modern culture at its best, no poverty, no drunkenness, no zymotic diseases, no crime, no police, only polite and refined and harmless people. Here was a middle-class paradise, kindergarten and model schools, lectures and classes and music, bicycling and swimming, and culture and kindness and elysian peace. But at the end of a week he came out into the real world, and he said:

Ouf! What a relief! Now for something primordial and savage, even though it were as bad as an Armenian massacre, to set the balance straight again. This order is too tame, this culture too second-rate, this goodness too uninspiring. This human drama, without a villain or a pang; this community so refined that ice-cream soda-water is the utmost offering it can make to the brute animal in man; this city simmering in the tepid lakeside sun; this atrocious harmlessness of all things—I cannot abide with them.

What men want, he says, is something more precipitous, something with more zest in it, with more adventure. Nearly all the utopias paint the life of the future as a kind of giant Chautauqua, in which every man and woman is at work, all are well fed, satisfied, and cultivated. But as man is now constituted he would probably find such a life flat, stale, and unprofitable.[8]

The appeal of utopias, like that of ideologies, rests on a special view of society. Yet even if the view they present

[7] Aldous Leonard Huxley, *Brave New World,* New York: Modern Library, 1946. George Orwell, *1984,* New York: Harcourt, Brace and Company, 1949. In paper: Signet 798.

[8] Robert E. Park and E. W. Burgess, *Introduction to the Science of Sociology,* Chicago: University of Chicago Press, 1924, pps. 598-599.

seems unrealistic, the consequences themselves may be real, and must be considered.[9]

Vilfredo Pareto and others have discussed the consequences of *myths* in society. "Myth" in this sense means a system of ideas (very often utopian) which are set up to inspire action. Pareto presented a graphical depiction of the operation of a myth, which with slight modification we reproduce.[10]

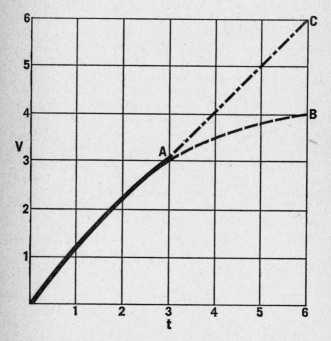

The solid line in the graph represents the past progress of the movement, and the broken lines extrapolate the probable future progress. The *t* dimension along the

[9] See, among others, Herbert J. Muller, *The Uses of the Past*, New York: The Oxford Press, Inc., 1952; also Mentor MS 112.
[10] Vilfredo Pareto, *The Mind and Society*, edited by Arthur Livingston, New York: Harcourt, Brace and Company, 1935 (four volumes). See pp. 1300 ff.

X axis can be days, months, years, or any other unit of time. The vertical dimension, *v*, represents units of some value (numbers of members, amount of money, acres of territory, etc.) At point *A* three years have passed and they have gathered three million dollars. A statistician would say that the rate of growth is diminishing, and that the next three years of similar effort are likely to bring them to point *B*—not very inspiring to the already tired and reasonably satisfied members. The leader may understand statistics but he wants the additional half million, and more than that, he wants to keep the movement going and in fighting trim; so he holds out the promise (*C*) of the same degree of reward in the next three years as has been gained in the past three.

Leaders frequently promise more than is realizable, thinking that the average follower would not work if he could foresee how little better off he will be even after a long struggle. It may be a sad commentary on human nature—both that we are unwilling to work hard for moderate betterment, and that we can be fooled into working for unobtainable goals, like greyhounds chasing a mechanical rabbit. Such, however, is the case. It is up to the leader to judge how far out to dangle the rabbit. Too close, and the dogs slow down. Too far, and they quit. Just far enough, and they run as hard as they can. And, the farther out the leader holds the rabbit, the bigger the rabbit must be.

These various bases of appeal and authority—*legitimacy, divinity, natural law, ideology* and *utopia,* and *myths*—may appear with varying degrees of formality. The least formal is implicit in the personal attraction of the charismatic leader. In their most formal presentation, they emerge as systematized philosophies. Which is more effective depends partly upon the kind of people to whom the movement must appeal and the degree of permanence which is sought for its structure. Christianity started as a movement centering around a single charismatic leader who lived simply and spoke plainly.

Gradually, the things he said began to crystallize for his followers so that they could teach them to others. By the time Christianity became the official church of the Roman Empire, a genuine philosophy had developed which reached a high point in the writings of St. Augustine and St. Thomas. This philosophy was not a mere adornment but a practical necessity if Christians were to argue successfully against the pagan philosophies of their day and persuade intellectuals to join the movement.[11]

Similarly Karl Marx and later writers developed a philosophy to back up Communism; even Adolph Hitler had his professional philosophers. So, too, several brilliant men contributed to the philosophies written to support the American and French revolutions. In short, men not only want to do things, they want to convince themselves and others that they are right in doing them, and philosophy is one of the intellectual tools for this job.

Organization

Although other parts of this book also consider aspects of organization, under this heading I wish to abstract several characteristics which provide a skeletal view of movements, apart from the details of membership, policy, and practice which are the meat on the bones. These characteristics of organization are *visibility, formality, types of meetings, leadership determination,* and *policy formation.*

a. *Visibility* has to do with the extent to which a movement's composition and activities are open to public inspection or hidden from general view. Is there an

[11] In connection with the relation between philosophy and the ideologies of political movements the reader may wish to consult Bertrand Russell, *Unpopular Essays,* New York: Simon and Schuster, 1950, especially the first essay, "Philosophy and Politics."

available membership list? Are financial reports subject to public scrutiny? Can anyone attend the meetings? Do members openly acknowledge their membership? Are the activities of the movement apparent to the public? If the answers to most of these and similar questions are "yes," the movement may be regarded as highly visible. If the answers are "no," the movement can be classified as clandestine or underground. Knowing whether a movement is visible or underground permits us to infer other facts about it.

First off, public opinion controls a visible movement more than one which is not—a redundant statement, of course, because if a movement goes underground it is probably because its policies and practices are such that the public would not accept them. If a movement is hiding, it probably has reason to hide. However, it is a mistake to conclude that any underground movement seeks the overthrow of the government, the perversion of the moral code, or the destruction of all nonmembers.

Most of us have at some time shivered to tales of black magic, spies, and Robin Hoods. Time and again movies have reiterated the theme of the beleaguered hero singlehandedly battling for good against powerful forces of intrigue. Certainly an imaginative and childlike desire to be big and powerful has accounted for some clandestine movements. The so-called "mysteries" of Rosicrucianism, I AM, the Masonic orders, and numerous quasi-religious movements spring partly from this motivation.

Some movements deal wholesale in dreams, professionally prepared for those who lack the craftsmanship to build their own. In a movement which pretends to a long and glorious history, members thrill in participating in hidden knowledge and ceremonies dating back to the warlocks and alchemists of old. They walk with Jurgen on Walpurgis Eve, celebrate ancient rituals with Moses Maimonides and Albertus Magnus, counsel in the night with Merlin, Nostradamus, and Benvenuto Cellini. They plot political intrigue with Richelieu and the Borgias, revel poetically with Cyrano and François Villon, fight beside Genghis Khan, Sir Henry Morgan, the Black Knight, and Frederick Barbarosa, and share romantic adventures with many another fictionalized personage of fame or dark repute. Mystery often is fun, and the shipping clerk whose psyche takes a beating every day from the boss and every night from his wife can compensate by poring over faded parchments and donning briefly the hallowed robes of the Great Grand Ghoul of the Seven Centers of Sinister Sophistry.

Some of this appeal also promotes movements which actually are subversive. In the previous chapter we noted how some young Americans in the 1930's were attracted to Communism in this way.

The casual exploitation of romantic youngsters is frequent among subversive movements. In the rather unsatisfactory world that young folk have been entering for several thousands of years, many things make for such an appeal. The narcotics problem stems in part from the same search for meaning by bewildered youth, as did drinking during prohibition days.

When one cannot see clearly enough to be *for* something he may assert his integrity by being against something. Many social movements offer things he can be against. As he ages the youngster may and often does become disenchanted with the movement either through wisdom, the attraction of a secure place in conservative society, the accumulation of responsibilities which no longer permit lighthearted adventuring, or just plain middle-aged fatigue. Meanwhile, however, some of his energies have served the movement.

A genuinely subversive movement may operate underground because this is effective strategy. A mystical movement may do so largely to preserve its appearance of mystery and exclusiveness. Avant-garde movements usually go underground only after unpleasant brushes with Philistines. Some simply don't want to bother with outsiders. Then, too, to some outsiders the reasons offered for secrecy by some movements seem delusory.

(The John Birch society claims that a dark conspiracy seeks to destroy the Birchers for their unusual patriotism, should their names be known. Apparently one must share this anxiety to join.) Finally, what is partially hidden often appears potentially dangerous, and a weak movement may conceal its numbers simply to pretend to more strength and influence than it actually commands.

b. A favorite dichotomy of sociologists is *formal* versus *informal* structure, and derivatively formal versus informal social control. As was indicated in discussing numbers, these two types of control are appropriate and effective in different size groups. By informal control, we simply mean that the authority to give and enforce commands which regulate conduct is personal, based on the intimate relations between people. If a man is well muscled, speaks persuasively, has piled up favors done for other people for which he can demand favors in return, or is just plainly well liked or well feared, he can exert informal control. Informal control appears as the casual friendly suggestion, the plea for assistance, the implied or open personal threat, the teasing, kidding, or barbed ridicule in a group, or the silent treatment of an erring member. The obvious advantage of informal control is that it can be applied whenever and wherever people get together. The disadvantage is that it won't always work, because it requires the assent of the person being controlled, and in some situations he can as readily withhold his assent as give it.

For this reason, large social movements almost invariably invoke formal controls. A common model for formal structure is that of the corporation, whose officers have special titles and stated responsibilities, with a considerable division of labor. This may be drawn up in a constitution, with by-laws appended, which every member is expected to know and respect, and actions are then taken in accord with the written formulas.

Just as informal does not mean accidental or spontaneous, formal does not mean deliberate. The words refer rather to the relative presence or absence of "forms" of behavior; that is to say, clearcut patterns which are describable, generally understood, and carefully observed. Often these forms are defined in words, systematically codified, and published. Examples include Roberts' Rules of Order, Army Regulations, or the Table of Organization of a military or commercial unit. In these the roles of the participants are clearly spelled out, the relationships of authority shown, and the channels of communication established, perhaps even including the "proper" attire for persons in certain roles, and the manner in which they are to be addressed by others.

An important question is whether the formal picture of the structure actually represents the way a movement works. The corporation is not necessarily the most appropriate model. Some ecclesiastical, parliamentary, or military model might have been more efficient. Or, perhaps the structure is simply too highly formalized, with a division of labor too complex for the job to be done. In such a case, the machinery gets in the way and work must be done by circumvention of official forms—a very likely situation if a movement adopts a formal structure early in its development. Tastes in structure are sometimes irrational, being colored by the emotions generated in past experiences. Thus men who did well in the army may prefer a military model, while men who hated the army may object to such a small thing as calling an official "sergeant," even if he is only "sergeant-at-arms." Businessmen approve Boards, Executive Secretaries, and expensive letterheads. Laborers may regard these with suspicion.

The formal structure pretends to define the channels of communication, but if use of these channels hinders communication, informal channels will develop, or control will break down, or both. Usually it is easier to change the *functions* of the movement piece by piece than it is to change the official *structure*, but obvious changes of function may cause friction and discontent. In effect, while social movements may seek some departure from the traditions of the culture, they are bound by their own traditions, as is all mankind. What we improvise today in an emergency remains tomorrow as a sacred precedent and the wisdom of the past. If traditions accumulate too quickly and are accorded too much respect, the frost may come before the flower. This is precisely the history of many unsuccessful social movements, which commit suicide by rigidly adhering to an immature and unprofitable design.

John Tsouderos compared ten voluntary associations such as the Y.M.C.A., labor organizations, and benevolent and protective orders and found a relationship between growth in membership and income, costs of administration, property, and number of paid staff. According to this study, membership tends to climb to a peak, level off for a while, and then decline. Income usually reaches its peak after the membership has already begun to decline. Costs of administration grow steadily with membership and income, but then increase rapidly after the income peaks. Property and staff continue to increase even after income begins to shrink. These sequences are explained by the change of structure as the organizations grow older. In the beginning, they are made up of highly motivated "amateurs," who give much time and enthusiasm, not all of which is integrated and directed. Later, formal machinery is established, which accounts in part for the rise in income, even though membership is stable or even falling: the professional staff is more efficient in collecting dues and in running fund raising campaigns. The observable efficiency leads the members to rely more and more upon the bureaucratic staff and less upon the enthusiastic amateur. When membership and income begin to shrink, they formalize even more in the attempt to maintain an organization which by now may have lost much of its original appeal. The congenial primary group of pioneers is now either gone or safely established in prestige positions and no longer experimenting with new ideas. What was once a glorious adventure has in effect become a reasonably efficient, but routine operation. The "movement" has become an "institution." [12]

c. The *type of meeting* held by a movement is related to the degree of formality in its structure. Movements modelled after business corporations tend to hold meetings like those of executive boards, with formal parliamentary procedures, careful attention to protocol, minutes, and secretarial reports. Other movements resemble more the old-fashioned camp meetings of evangelical religious sects. Some display ostentatious pomp and solemnity, bordering on the magical. Others suggest folksy picnic suppers or ice cream socials. If it can be assumed that the form of meeting has been deliberately and rationally selected by the leaders, we can infer something about the roles which the leaders expect their followers to take in the organization.

In describing the banquet meetings of Father Divine, for example, Cantril indicated that Father wanted his children to eat, celebrate, and adore, but not to think or criticize or attempt to form organization policies. Banquets promote unity and warm feeling, but not critical discussion. The Nazi mass meetings implied different expectations. A show of strength to impress the public, iron discipline evidenced by precision drill, spine-tingling martial music and drum beats—all of these indicated that the follower was expected to be eagerly obedient and severely orthodox in every action. How different both of these are from the collective meditation of a group of Friends, who follow no strong leader but rather sit quietly together, waiting for the inspiration which may come to any sincere member for the guidance of all.

Preferring a discussion technique reflects a democratic bias, which is not necessarily good or bad, but one that

[12] John E. Tsouderos, Georgia Institute of Technology, "Organizational Change in Terms of a Series of Selected Variables," paper read at national convention of American Sociological Society, 1954, Urbana, Illinois.

should be recognized. It assumes that the leader is not a figure of authority or an expert, but rather that decisions must be made by the whole group, after interchange of ideas. Each person in the group is assumed to share in the authority and expertness required to meet the problem at hand. If this assumption is true, and if the problem is one vitally affecting each member, then this form of meeting is reasonably appropriate. However, meeting forms are not usually chosen so self-consciously and deliberately.

Most intelligent people observe the difficulties in controlling others, and many of us envy those few people who show great skill in handling a group. Thus any technique which skilled men define may be used by people without training, talent, or willingness to work. And just as some followers join social movements which hand them ready-made dreams of wisdom and power, so some leaders snatch at control gimmicks, push-button psychologies which promise quick and easy solutions to the problems of group organization.

The results are what one might expect. If the situation, the problem, and the personnel are suitable, and the leader is reasonably talented, satisfactory results are obtained. If one or more of these conditions is not met, results are less satisfactory. If all are wrong, the result is miserable failure. Lacking a sound theoretical understanding of what is supposed to occur and how, people often doggedly adhere to the formula for a time, then losing faith after spotty success and frequent failure, they become exasperated with the gimmick and reject it as worthless; whereas, in fact, it was a perfectly good tool if only it had been applied properly to do a specific job.

Regardless of the merits of any special system for running a meeting, the opposing forces of novelty and tradition must always be considered and weighed. Some groups are used to and approve of traditional forms, so that use of them gives assurance and confidence in the propriety of what is being done (for example, starting with a prayer and the reading of minutes). On the other hand, new forms may suggest that new ideas will succeed, and in this way generate enthusiasm. Moreover, since people who join social movements are frequently dissatisfied with old-fashioned ways of doing things, a change in form as well as in purpose pleases many, so long as the movement is getting along well otherwise.

Novelty is generally more acceptable to young people than to old. The Oxford Group, in appealing to young people, offered them religion in a house party at which they could let down their hair and discuss religious and moral problems intimately. This was much like the old-fashioned testimonial or confessional meeting of many Protestant churches years before, but it was cast in a new and "sophisticated" setting. Its effectiveness came in part from letting people who thought they were sophisticated do something very naive and still feel very sophisticated in the process. The Townsend Plan, on the other hand, appealing largely to older people, reassured them that its revolutionary ideas were quite respectable and sound because the form of meeting the clubs held was patterned after old-fashioned church meetings. In other words revolutionary aims may be implemented in a conservative way, or conservative aims in a revolutionary way, depending in part upon the tastes you wish to respect.

This last generalization carries beyond the type of meeting to all symbolic aspects of the movement. It is especially important in assessing the meaning and attractiveness of radical movements. Under the guise of conservative patriotism, for example, a movement may actually preach highly reactionary or revolutionary doctrines, and many members who are attracted by the frequent references to God, the Flag, Motherhood, and Morality never realize that should the movement succeed many of their own basic values would go by the board. So, too, under the guise of idealism a movement may promote base purposes. The Ku Klux Klan has claimed Protestantism, when on inspection it appears not so much to favor Protestant Christianity as to oppose Catholicism, Judaism, and most racial and ethnic minorities. The Minute Women, taking their name from a romantic and heroic group of men in the Revolutionary War period, claim to be saviors of democracy, but in effect their policies and actions closely parallel European fascism. The John Birchers are so patriotic they dare not even let ordinary citizens know what they are doing. The Communists' demands for civil rights are by now transparent.

d. The role of the follower can be inferred from the type of meeting which the group employs. We may also infer from this the role of the *leader,* how he is selected, and how other leaders may be recruited. If the organization is democratic, a new leader or leaders may emerge at any time, depending upon the current problems and the feelings of the group. In an informal meeting, a leader may arise simply by volunteering to do a piece of work, or people may casually suggest that he do so. Often, the process is so smooth and gradual that it is difficult to say just when the authority changed hands.

We should not infer from this that only informal groups may be democratic. If the formal structure is well planned and the procedures agreeable to the members (which is another way of saying that the official channels of communication function smoothly), leaders may be selected and other business may be done democratically, even though red tape is used.

In considering authority and appeal we noted Max Weber's three types of leadership, based on different notions of what makes authority socially legitimate. Thus a traditional leader might obtain his position by descent from his father or from some other relative who had led the group, or perhaps be appointed by the previous leader to replace him. "What has been" determines what is to be." Bureaucratic leaders hold authority by legal right, typically established in an accepted constitution, and their recruitment may come through election or appointment on the basis of tests. Charismatic leaders achieve power through personal appeal. A man who is outstanding in valor, speech making, miracle working, or divine inspiration, may be hailed as a leader although he has neither traditional right nor legal sanction.

Christ is the preeminent example of a charismatic leader, but many leaders of lesser appeal can also be cited as falling in this category. Joseph Smith of the Mormons, Father Divine, Adolf Hitler, Father Coughlin, all had the charismatic touch. It is worth noting that charisma, like magic, appeals only while it gets results. No one is less respected than the charismatic leader who fails. Even Christ lost most of his following when he was crucified, and only by the hard work of a few men whom he had greatly moved did Christianity survive.

If a movement is avowedly antitraditional, or has no immediate traditional base of support, or if its potential leaders and followers lack economic or other social power, the leadership is likely to be charismatic. However, if the other kinds of power are available, they are more dependable and are apt to be used. No wise leader, even if he does have the touch of charisma, will let his leadership rest very long on a purely charismatic base, simply because at the first slip he may lose his control.

Leadership of movements often proceeds rapidly from charisma to legal or traditional authority. Consequently, after a number of successes, when he wants support for some new venture, the leader may ask "Haven't I always brought you through all right? Have you ever lost out by following me? Just have a little more faith. We have a hard road ahead, but the same success I have given you in the past will be yours again." He is attempting to elicit traditional thinking. "Don't change horses in the middle of the stream," "Tried and true," and similar expressions from folklore support the traditional figure. If the movement takes a parliamentary form, there are legalistic supports to retain power.

Adolf Hitler, a charismatic leader at the start, used both legal and traditional institutions to insure power.

Max Weber writes of the "charisma of office," or how
the halo which once shone over a superior man may attach in part to the position he held. Respect which was
given the first king for his personal virtues may later be
given a vastly inferior descendant merely because he
bears the title. Howard Becker shows how such transfer-
ence occurred in the German youth movement. The
early leaders held their followers by sheer personal
power. Later, Hitler appointed a leader who probably
could not have competed with these earlier men but
who still received some of the respect which the charismatic leaders had aroused.[13]

Vilfredo Pareto described power as passing typically
from the lions to the foxes.[14] By this he meant that the
strong, hungry, ruthless men who carved out a throne
for themselves by courageous violence, did so only to be
succeeded by cautious men who substituted clever
scheming for reckless daring. These foxes were then
often overthrown by later lions. Although the formula is
a little too simple, there is some truth in it. Conditions
surrounding a movement, and the structure of the
movement itself, do change over time. Forms which are
appropriate in the beginning may require later modification, and so too what is appropriate leadership changes.
A leader who is well qualified to initiate a movement
often proves to be a serious handicap when the movement becomes established. Many a stirring evangelist
makes a poor pastor. Either the leader must change
himself, or the leader must be changed.

The window-smashing, bone-breaking violence that
attended the formation of some of the American labor
unions was totally unsuitable to conference-table diplomacy with government and management once the union

[13] Howard Becker, *German Youth, Bond or Free,* New York:
Oxford University Press, 1946.
[14] Vilfredo Pareto, *The Mind and Society,* edited by Arthur
Livingston, New York: Harcourt, Brace and Company, 1935
(four volumes). See p. 2178 ff. *et passim.* For discussion, see
Talcott Parsons, *The Structure of Social Action,* New York:
McGraw-Hill Book Company, 1937, pp. 278 ff.

changed from a social movement to an institution. Some
union leaders changed; others were replaced. Marcus
Garvey in the 1920's established a social movement but
could not adequately manage its affairs. And in the
1940's Henry Wallace attracted many people sufficiently
for them to follow him in his several shifts of policy. But
while he appeared to many followers as a forthright
righteous, and inspired man, he lacked the technique:
necessary to run a political party. Both Garvey and Wal
lace experienced a resounding collapse.

If a movement matures slowly, leadership may
change appropriately as a process of maturing. A young
tough, venturesome personal leader may grow into his
middle years as a sober, conservative executive. Fre
quently, however, social movements emerge, expand
and run their course before the leader can reshape hi
personality to fit the demands. He is often too young o
too old. Or, to put it in another frame of reference
many a leader has talent but no technique. Unless h
disciplines himself to self-conscious, deliberate, rationa
exploitation of his abilities, the leader usually canno
compete with other men, equally talented but better o
ganized, and his movement is often taken from him o
destroyed. Technique in leading human beings is har
won.

Not all leaders, of course, are rational and systemati
Some are opportunists who develop to a high art th
ability to land on their feet after each upset. Othe
suffer pathologically from some *idée fixe* or single ove
simplified idea which they pursue without regard fo
their chances of success. Most of the latter are shunne
by society as cranks, or locked up when they depart fa
enough from accepted practices, but some live to see th
mores change around them so that they become "righ
and can claim vision and insight and a wisdom beyon
that of ordinary men.

A leader wise enough to foresee the future may l
impatient with the present and not "well adjusted
What history may later call his great vision and persis

ence is likely in his own time to be reckoned as irritability and stubbornness. Externally, reasoned indignation looks about the same as bad manners. Anger alone never attests to cosmic purpose, and many leaders of social movements of widely diverse purposes are "angry young men." In the long run, greatness is a historical judgment of events, and adjustment the psychological accounting of inner states. The historical and psychological assessments are not totally unrelated, but it is hardly profitable to insist on their comparison.

e. Usually the manner in which *policy* is determined is related to the selection of leaders. A charismatic leader ordinarily determines policy himself or with the aid of close associates. This also may be true of traditional or bureaucratic leaders, but here other possibilities are open. Bureaucratic leaders, for example, may be executives who carry out policies determined by others, and traditional leaders may be figureheads. If leaders are chosen democratically, policy may be determined in the same way. In movements where the leader exercises a stern and remote control over the policies and where local units of the larger movement get their orders and their current "line" from the top down, a study of the organization's policies may approximate a psychiatric study of the leader himself. Men with great power sometimes give large expressions to small whims.

Certainly it is astounding how little the followers in some movements know about their leaders and the policies which they so abjectly obey. For instance, one of my students found people in the Jehovah's Witnesses who believed that their instructions still came from their beloved leader, Judge Rutherford, unaware that he had died six years before. To most of the flock, he was only a book or pamphlet or a phonograph record, and since the materials which he had produced were still being used, these followers thought him alive.

Movements which attempt a strong and remote control over members sometimes publish indexes of banned reading material, discourage education, and breed suspicion of outsiders so that followers will not communicate sympathetically with any person or group who might start them thinking critically about the policies of the movement. "Believe; do not question." "Feel; do not think." "Love; do not measure."

Unity and Continuity

In order to stay together long enough to change society, a social movement must be planned and organized. We will discuss some of the many techniques which help to hold people together and keep them operating consistently and effectively.

a. *Identifying symbols.* We have already noted the symbolic importance of different types of meetings in setting an emotional tone and implying to members their proper roles. Other symbols identify the members to one another and to outsiders as well. If the leader is charismatic, such identifying symbols can be borrowed directly from his personal appearance or from his preferences in gesture or dress. We must appreciate the reverence which the followers hold for the leader before we can assess the importance of these symbols to them. Hitler's little mustache seemed comic to Americans, but to many Germans it stood for Teutonic masculine superiority and was a badge of greatness. It was a good symbol because most German men could grow a duplicate, and many did.

The force of such symbols is sometimes ironically amusing, because the leader who has been so symbolized is compelled to sustain them, whether he wants to or not.

Take the case of Dizzy Gillespie, one of the leaders in the Bop movement in American Jazz in the 1940's. Dizzy wore horn-rimmed spectacles to improve his sight, a small goatee to help his trumpet lip, and a beret, largely as a convenience. When the Bop movement arose around him these things became symbols of the group;

yet it was hard to defend such symbols rationally. A mustache or goatee may strengthen a brass or reed player's embouchure (debatable!), but why should a drummer or piano man wear one? Glasses may be required, but why horn rims? And as for the beret, it is a useful hat but so are others. As a matter of fact, a profile in *The New Yorker*[15] reported that Gillespie became enamored of a miner's cap while playing a dance in the coal fields and wanted to wear one until one of his supporters argued him out of it, shrewdly insisting that dropping the symbol would weaken his hold on the other boppers. The same story reports French trumpet men banging dents in their horns because Dizzy happened to play some tour engagements with a travel-worn instrument. Symbols, in short, are irrational perhaps, but influential. What is so attractive about an elephant or a donkey? Is a swastika or a crescent intrinsically aesthetic? How many national flags are works of art?

Badges, special uniforms, handshaking "grips," automobile stickers, anything which is available and economically practical for members can be established as a symbol of organization. If the symbol carries with it a slight amount of utility, it will become even stronger. After all, a man has to wear some sort of a haircut unless he is bald, so musicians of one era could defend long hair as looking better on the stage or under strong lighting, and later musicians could defend crew-cuts as convenient when making road trips, but in both cases a principal function was identification. In a climate where one wears a hat much of the time it is not hard to establish some particular hat as the mark of the member. Nearly every kind has been chosen to represent some movement: tricorn, fez, top hat, derby, cap, beret, ten gallon, or slouch.

A leader who seeks to make himself known does well to distinguish himself in some part of his dress, espe-

[15] Richard O. Boyer, "Profiles: Bop," *The New Yorker,* July 3, 1948, pp. 26 ff.

cially if the distinguishing mark has the refreshing air of
shunning outworn formality for present utility. Such was
the Ike jacket and the Prince of Wales soft shirt. Some
symbols are chosen not to be imitated but rather respected, as, for example, in World War II General Mac-
Arthur's famous scrambled-eggs cap or General Patton's
revolvers. It is a real question just how far a general
should go in presenting himself as a "character." Some
undoubtedly go too far, but bravado and symbol-
waving are necessary to build the notion of a personal
leader in an army where standardization is the keynote.
The same holds true in a social movement, which must
dramatize and symbolize its differences from the rest of
the culture. The eagerness with which soldiers, condemned by edict and custom to a uniform dress, seize
upon scarves, specialized regalia, unusual shoes, and the
like simply underlines in an extreme situation this tendency, which may be observed elsewhere in society.

The limits to the choices of symbols are broad and
loose. Out-and-out obscenity is usually unacceptable.
Effeminacy cannot be courted by most groups appealing
to men. Scarification of the body or face, while not appealing to most civilized adults, does sometimes appeal
to youngsters, for whom scars symbolize violent and
presumably laudable experience. Yet even rules like
these are tenuous. To be sure, symbols must not diamet-
rically oppose the values the followers bring with them
to the movement. But beyond this, almost anything
goes. Secret, and especially subversive, social movements use symbols which deliberately do not communicate to the general public, but which carry meanings between members. A humorous example is the "distress
signal" found in fraternal orders, by which a brother in
trouble can appeal to another. A more serious situation
occurs when a movement spreads widely but secretly so
that members who must make contact in order to do
their work cannot openly recognize each other.

This latter problem has been faced by the Commuists, the anti-Nazi underground, and similar groups. In such instances the symbol which is chosen must be intrinsically innocuous, something that anyone might ordinarily carry about with him, but which cannot be readily apprehended and counterfeited by the opposition—a spot of dirt on a particular part of a shoe; the offer of cigarets from a case in which two preselected brands may be seen; display of a piece of paper money with a serial number falling within a certain series; the nervous habit of biting a certain fingernail; use of a special word in a way which is meaningless to outsiders. A standard trick is to take a stamp, a picture, a piece of newspaper, or a piece of paper money and tear it jaggedly in half, giving one piece to each of the two persons who are to rendezvous. Duplication of the token is virtually impossible unless you have one of the pieces, but this artifice is so well known that even finding a man with half of something looks suspicious. If there is danger of interception, other less obvious devices are preferred. For such cloak and dagger occasions any object, word, or action may be used as a code, providing one has time to set it up in advance.

When code symbols must be improvised on the spur of the moment, ingenious use of the subculture of the group has often provided an answer. The Bible gives us the term "shibboleth," a word which the Ephraimites and the Gileadites pronounced differently. This term applies to any special test word, password, or party slogan which is important not so much for itself as for the categoric differences it identifies. Eating with the right or left hand, lighting matches in a certain way, tamping or not tamping a cigaret before lighting it, all of these things have tripped up some spies and admitted others when they were used as shibboleths. It is very difficult, however, for a man to remold all of his personality to the pattern of some other group, even if he is astute enough to perceive the pattern; thus, any shrewd observer can usually detect the stranger if he tries hard enough. Not only the word, and the context of the word, but even the inflection itself, may distinguish the true member from the pretender.

b. *Oaths and creeds.* Since a social movement is concerned with collecting people and instrumenting an idea, it is of the utmost importance that this idea be shared by all of the members. Ideas, however, are intangible and easily become distorted from their original form. Consequently, if a social movement is to maintain unity and continuity from one time to another and from one person to another, part of the central idea must somehow be frozen to provide a common core of thought around which mediation, discussion, and work will dependably center. This often takes the form of oaths or creeds.

Several purposes are served by oaths and creeds. In the beginning of a social movement, it is difficult to be certain that all of the professed members are interested in the same goals. It is hard too to be sure how much devotion and obedience can be commanded from those who are presumably interested. Some formal statement of contract supporting the leader and the movement in its policies and its practical actions thus becomes handy. Creeds provide a formal statement of belief; usually not a complete statement, but a generally acceptable one. A thumbnail sketch of an ideology, a creed is the symbol of a whole collection of other symbols, and serves to mark out basic points of agreement among members. In its interpretation, of course, there may be differences among the members, and in this respect the symbol is like shorthand notes, which mean approximately the same to anyone who knows the system, but which are subject to some individual interpretation at the hands of particular stenographers. Yet ambiguity in creeds may be useful in permitting a restricted freedom of thought to the members, while assuring that basically they agree.

Just as creeds provide a formal statement of belief, so

oaths provide a formal statement of duties and obligations. In agreeing to a creed, a man acknowledges be-
liefs. In taking an oath he promises behavior. On the
basis of the creed the oath is acceptable, and without at
least the implicit acceptance of a creed the oath may not
be psychologically binding.

Obviously both of these devices are artificial attempts
to create unity, and would be unnecessary if unity already existed. Thus it is to be expected that they will
often be abused and sometimes completely fail, especially if they degenerate into ritualistic observances
which have no external force behind them to back them
up. The form of oaths makes this difficulty clear. "Cross
my heart and hope to die," "Upon my honor," and "Do
you solemnly swear. . . ," each poses an unanswered
question. If the person truly hopes to die, if he regards
his honor as something as dear as his life, if he believes
in God and takes his salvation or damnation seriously,
then chances are that such an oath will invoke considerable self-control and will direct his behavior. But suppose he does not—what then? Our courts of law regard
the oath as a form which permits us to invoke external
penalties if we can prove that the witness has perjured
himself. A bond mainly insures economically against his
departure.

Oaths are generally used in situations where we need
to trust each other and don't quite do so. References to
the beard of the prophet, the wounds of Christ, our
sainted ancestors, and other sacred symbols are psychological threats which may work for a time, but by frequent use may become debased, just as profanity loses
its impact when too often repeated. In short, we cannot
depend on the emotions which the symbols are intended
to arouse. Anyone who has learned a foreign language
after childhood finds that the denotative meanings are
there for him but do not carry the same feeling as his
native tongue. He can readily say things in his second
language that he would blush to utter in his first. Even

when he knows that words are taboo in the new language, he knows this by rote as he knows the multiplication table—he doesn't really feel it.

Other effects of oaths may be noted. People who regard their loyalty as proven and indisputable may resent compulsory "allegiance" oaths. On the other hand, oath-taking has a ritual value in that it publicly proclaims our solemn obedience to the values and authorities we accept. In having our school children pledge allegiance to the flag we do not ordinarily suspect them of treason or sabotage. Nor do the marriage vows necessarily imply intended infidelity. The question of honor comes up only when the oath is regarded as a *test of loyalty*, and where only certain groups are so tested.

c. *Fiscal Policy*. Social movements usually cost money, and as with any organization money can be spent more systematically if the income can be planned. Typical ways of obtaining money include dues, contributions, levies and assessments, collections, pledges, and endowments.

The least systematic method is to take up a collection. This does not mean that no techniques are involved, but simply that the income obtained is less predictable than with some other methods. Churches have long used the collection or "free will offering," as do groups having church background, such as some of the evangelical social movements. Its effectiveness depends largely on the skills of the leader and the emotional tone he creates prior to the "passing of the plate." Strong appeals sometimes transform the "free will offering" into a shake-down. Pitting one side of the audience against another, appealing to God to help find the little lady out there with a ten dollar bill in her purse, dramatically counting the money, identifying the large and the small giver, and then repeating the whole process "While we sing another stanza of our glorious anthem," are just a few of such devices. Praise and shame are wielded with huck-sterous candor by many leaders, some of whom are unabashed because of their sincerity and others through cold calculations of the profits.

A step away from the public collection is the private door-to-door, person-to-person appeal. This may be handled by the leader himself but is more often organized as a "drive," with followers going out singly or in pairs, approaching neighbors, friends, or even strangers on the street for gifts to keep the movement going. Buttons, stickers, or other little mementoes given in exchange serve the triple purpose of giving something tangible to the giver, showing the public who has been touched, and protecting the giver from being approached again immediately by the same group.

Other groups, less pressed financially or more conservative in their behavior, may simply depend upon unsolicited contributions. Yet the line between a contribution and a collection is dim indeed, and often subjective. Like the distinction between social control and self control it is often a question of whether one feels external pressure. If a man thinks he gives through his own volition, he calls it a contribution. If he gives when someone else prods him, he deems it a collection. If the prodder is subtle, he may still regard it as a contribution, and this term offers him more self-esteem.

In formally organized movements the commonest technique of fund raising is to charge dues, which every member is expected to pay before he is registered, and for which he receives explicit items and services. He receives a membership card, his name appears on the mailing list for announcements of meetings, he is authorized to vote in elections, he is sent the official publications, and enjoys reduced rates at some public affairs. And to some people these tangible symbols are a selling point.

Many organizations which seek fairly large sums from their members request annual pledges. This procedure recognizes the systematic organization of our economy, especially among salaried persons, who may not handle a great deal of money at any one time but who can predict with near certainty how much they will receive in the coming year. With pledges the leaders can also predict income for the year, collecting installments at the time when it has to be spent. Moreover, the businesslike and dignified nature of this procedure elicits more money from people who respect systematic methods, because its formality suggests a wise husbanding of the funds. (These same people may balk at giving to public collections.) Actually, of course, this does not logically follow and may reflect a middle-class bias.

If the movement has a great hold on the followers, with strong social and self controls, levies and assessments can be used. That is to say, the leaders simply announce what the members are to give, sometimes with amounts graduated to fit incomes, or classes of membership.

In sternly disciplined groups a minor source of income is obtained from fines and forfeitures, but these more commonly serve as punishments. A less common plan is endowment, wherein one man or a few underwrite the expenses of the movement and take upon themselves most of the financial burden of the other members. This plan may look desirable to the leader who is scuffling for money but it has serious shortcomings. For example, endowers often want to direct expenditures and wealth does not necessarily correlate with brains. Some men try to buy control of a movement, which otherwise they could not manage, and when this occurs a fight for power frequently follows. Deeper than this, when the rank and file do not pay for the movement's operations they may ignore the operations themselves, assuming simply that "George will do it." Others become "talking liberals" with free advice and fine words but no commitment. It is thus often a good test and a blow for unity for the leader to tell his followers flatly, "Put your money where your mouth is." Not only does this weed out laggardly fellow travelers, but it makes the contributing members more determined to see that they get something for their money, which usually means they will do more work.

Large and successful social movements may employ all of these devices upon occasion, tailoring each to fit immediate needs.

d. *Education and propaganda within the movement.* Creeds and oaths provide basic formulations of the ideas the movement stands for, but for these to have full meaning for the members, continuous education and propaganda must be carried on within the movement— to reiterate its fundamental purposes, to maintain the structure of authority, and to develop the techniques which will instrument the purposes. Many situations facilitate cultivation of members, ranging from informal chats with the leaders, through discussion groups organized for various levels of members, to formal academic instruction.

Some general problems and solutions to these problems can be observed. In any group engaged in social action people are usually distributed along a range of awareness and commitment. Some are willing to act recklessly while others are temporizing and cautious. The problem is to keep them in harmonious contact, while permitting each to contribute as best he can and where he will be the most effective.

The simplest way to do this—to use a military analogy —is to establish echelons of people and activities. Some people, by choice, or by necessity, must be the front line scouts, who take great chances and are expendable. Others, further back, must wait until the line of conflict becomes clear and then deploy to meet it. Still others must be held in reserve to meet later emergencies, and others must not be used directly at all but kept apart, observing, correlating, and planning so that loss of a single skirmish or even a major battle will not destroy the entire movement.

The echelon plan may be considered also with regard for the language employed. Just as few generals talk the language of privates, so too a man wise enough and well enough educated to make a good staff man often makes a poor field man. (Adlai Stevenson suffered this handicap as a presidential candidate. His speeches made excellent literature but did not appeal to a majority of voters.) Here again organizing various levels of people may provide a solution, and precisely as in a well run military unit. The man at the top can think, plan, and communicate effectively with his immediate inferiors. These men, in turn, can talk to those below them. The men at the bottom and the top may not be able to converse meaningfully, but if good communication is maintained between adjacent levels in the organization, properly translated information will travel up and down the line. Sergeants translate for enlisted men what the officer said, and explain to the officer what the reaction meant.

A frequent failing of movements interested in social action is their insistence on fighting from only one position, or using only one level of personnel. This has often been the case with movements supporting civil rights for Negroes in America. Some want immediate "radical" action. Others prefer to build friendships and congenial relations with conservative groups in the society on the basis of present conditions, and hope to effect moderate changes gradually. The various organizations present a spectrum, but communication between them is incomplete, and they often work at cross purposes and bicker among themselves.

Any movement which commits this sort of organizational error is wide open to the divide-and-conquer strategies of its enemies, as the Communists and other astutely combative movements know. An effectively organized social movement thus makes it a part of its educational program to show the members the range of roles they can play, clarify the conditions under which different tactics are to be used, and condition members to accept these different roles when they are called upon to do so. What to do, why to do it, and how to do it successfully must be the foci of education within the movement.

Beyond the practical tactical training and theoretical indoctrination of members, education and propaganda within the movement serve other purposes. The leader must seem to lead. In order to lead, he must appear to be a little ahead of his followers, a little wiser, a little more informed. But if he gets out too far ahead, contact is broken and he may become a "leader" without followers. The classic story in this regard describes a radical French politician sitting at a sidewalk cafe chatting with a friend; when an angry mob rushed down the street he excused himself hastily, saying, "There go my followers—I must lead them." If the followers are allowed to direct their attention and efforts on their own, without at least token leadership, the structure crumbles, and authority changes. Most successful leaders recognize this fact and persistently try to attract attention and to keep their people thinking about them.

Speeches, pageants, parades, and festivals lend themselves very well to keeping the leader on stage center. The Nazi Party exploited these devices on a massive scale. In George Orwell's *1984* [16] Big Brother is constantly watching everyone, and the Party members find every minute carefully planned and regulated so that it is virtually impossible to think about anything but Party business. Orwell intentionally makes his point by satiric exaggeration, but to a considerable extent such procedures are used in totalitarian countries. Given sufficient resources, it is possible to so effectively propagandize a group that few of its members can defect from the faith. The great majority of them are simply too busy, too restricted, and too overwhelmed by the constant insistence upon unanimity to criticize or rebel. Few American social movements achieve such monolithic control.

One ramification of propaganda—the "smoke-screen"

[16] George Orwell, *1984*, New York: Harcourt, Brace and Company, 1949. In paper: Signet 798.

technique—can be seen in many parts of our society today. If the leader can constantly irritate his people, even
with "smoke-screen" accusations which do not bear up
under critical scrutiny, he can arouse emotions. Part of
this annoyance may even be directed initially at him,
but if he can make himself appear invulnerable to attacks, the populace will vent its spleen elsewhere, often
at the very men he has scurrilously attacked.

This procedure is frightening to observe. There need
be *no* truth whatsoever to the original charges, although
a slight factual support does no harm. If the smoke-
screen is dense enough, people will convince themselves
that there is a fire behind it—if only to excuse their own
fears.[17]

In 1965 in Selma, Alabama, die-hard segregationists
sought to discredit the volunteers who came from outside to support freedom marchers by insisting that they
were Communists, and that they were generally engaged in illicit and interracial sexual intercourse.

Obviously, an isolated group can be more easily ma-
nipulated than one which encounters competing ideas
and interests. Most social movements seek to instill conviction, not objectivity. Moreover, modification of the
members' personalities can be more effectively accomplished if they can be trained in *isolation,* where they
are not permitted to live half in the movement and half
out. With volunteers, this isolation may be harder to

---

[17] Techniques of legitimate propaganda and "promotion" shade
imperceptibly into manipulation of information and on to outright
deceit. At this latter end we find movements which are only dis-
tinguishable from confidence games by courtesy of the definition.
Moreover, something can be learned about motivation from an
examination of confidence men whose livelihood depends upon
it. Four useful books are: Alexander Klein, *Grand Deception,*
Philadelphia: J. B. Lippincott Company, 1955; Alexander Klein,
The Double Dealers, Philadelphia: J. B. Lippincott Company,
1958; David W. Maurer, *The Big Con,* New York: The New
American Library, 1962; and Curtis D. MacDougall, *Hoaxes,*
New York: Dover Publications, 1958. See also biographies of
Wilson Mizner, "Soapy" Smith, and "Yellow Kid" Weil.

come by. Some powerful and well-financed movements can afford to support a man away from home while they indoctrinate him, but most cannot. In this case a second best approach is temporary isolation, such as is seen in the camp meeting or vacation retreat, both used by Hitler, for example. This offers only part of the advantage of the longer isolation, but with less interruption of everyday life, and at considerably less expense.

Whether retreats or other isolated training schools are needed depends on how much change of personality is required—how different the full-fledged member must be from the newly hatched recruit. The greater the difference, the more desirable the isolation. A certain ivory tower quality must obtain in any school which seeks fundamental changes in people's thinking.

As with other education and propaganda, any available communication devices can be used—books, pamphlets, occasional literature, official organs and periodic publications, radio, cinema, stage, or television, although the cost of the latter media exceeds the resources of most social movements.

e. *Discipline.* Some movements attempt strong and extensive control over their members, and most face at some time the problem of correcting misbehavior, checking destructive actions, and ultimately silencing or ousting troublemakers. Disciplinary techniques vary widely, but most of these are familiar from other social contexts and can be treated briefly.

Discipline is usually thought of as the result of suppressive actions, such as fines, imprisonment, corporal punishment, and death. These punishments are the *negative sanctions*, the positive being rewards. Penologists have shown that it is easier to find punishments which will apply to everyone in a nearly equal way than it is to find equally applying rewards, and it is often cheaper. But discipline based on punishments can only be maintained when the movement has authority that is generally respected. Then, too, it is always uncertain how much of a beating a man will take from a movement which he has joined voluntarily. Severe punishment may make him drop out.

One common technique is to keep a list, available to members, of those who have done well or poorly in important activities. These rosters, "gig sheets," and blacklists serve the double purpose of rewarding or punishing the individual member by publicizing his activity to the others, while at the same time exerting a constant pressure on the others to keep their names on or off the list. The blacklist technique culminates in ostracism or excommunication. The so-called "silent treatment," wherein a man is punished by having everyone refuse to talk to him, is a secular excommunication applied in small isolated groups. Obviously its effect depends upon the degree to which the man needs the group; if other groups are accessible, he may turn to them.

In brief, punishments deprive a man of property or pleasure, or restrict his action. The maximum severity of the punishments is limited by the ability of the movement to monopolize the experiences of the members.

Positive sanctions may take any form the members will accept and respond to: awards and citations, honorific titles, promotions, and "dividends" in the form of jobs, banquets, booty, and special privileges. To the extent that members resemble other people in their society, the positive controls used to entice and attract them will be similar to those used outside, but, in addition, the movement may provide opportunity for actions which the rest of society restricts. For example, the main activity of nudism, appearing semipublicly with no clothes on, seems for some to be a reward in itself. Even in movements with less exotic purposes "forbidden fruit" may be offered as an attraction to people who do not find the main purposes glamorous.

In this chapter we have examined some salient and persistent characteristics of social movements which are similar to those defining other social groups. These fall into three broad categories: those which provide a rationale for the movement, those which define the general pattern of communication within the movement, and those which perpetuate the first two. These categories were captioned as follows: bases of authority and appeal, organization, and unity and continuity. It might strike a naive observer as inconsistent that a group of people who are intent on changing the world should be bound by rules. This problem is inherent in much of Western thought, and usually discussed under the rubric of "freedom." However, as there is not time or space to develop the argument here, it must be simply asserted that all effective action demands "structure" or stable organization, and actions directed at change demand more self-conscious organization than actions which merely repeat well-established cultural processes. Success or failure of social movements in changing the culture or social order often depends greatly on organizational skill. Whether organization is rationally planned, or accidentally emerges is perhaps immaterial, but the suitability of organization to the problem is crucial. A movement which struggled along for years before finding appropriate structures and techniques of action is the Civil Rights movement among American Negroes. A brief description of this example follows.

An Example: The Civil Rights Movement

by James H. Laue[18]

The drive for equal rights among Negro Americans in the last decade offers an unprecedented living laboratory for the study of spontaneity and institutionalization in an on-going social movement. Beginning with the 1954 Supreme Court decision barring public school segregation, a growing consciousness of strength and unity of purpose have crystallized into one of the most wide-

[18] Adapted from: "Direct Action and Desegregation: A Study in Social Spontaneity and Institutionalization," by James H. Laue, a doctoral dissertation completed for the Department of Social Relations, Harvard University, 1965.

spread and successful social movements in American history.

As in many movements, the desegregation drive has fluctuated between spontaneous, uncoordinated protests (those in the direct action movement call these "spectaculars") and planned, formal approaches to the problem ("getting down to the knitty-gritty"). But while both have contributed to the long strides toward equal opportunity for Negroes in recent years, the sense of "movement" which has developed since 1960 is directly tied to the openly charismatic activities of the sit-inners, Freedom Riders, and voting workers in Deep South states.

A BRIEF HISTORY OF PROTEST

Pre-1954—Before the Supreme Court ruling in 1954, the approach of desegregation strategists was basically educational and legal. Lawyers for the National Association for the Advancement of Colored People waged a twenty year series of court cases culminating in the famous *Brown vs. Board of Education* Supreme Court decision of May 17, 1954. Low educational levels, lack of economic and political power, and the resulting scarcity of articulate Negro leadership had necessarily kept the drive for equal rights in the hands of a few skilled professionals. A major goal, legal desegregation of schools, had been achieved, but no one talked of a "school desegregation movement."

1955-60—Suddenly the elements needed for a broad-based social movement in Negro America came together in Montgomery, Alabama. Here was born a simple and understandable goal, a religiously sanctioned philosophy, a strategy of action, a charismatic leader, and a new-found sense of the power of mass action. The goal was first come, first served on bus seats. The philosophy was Gandhian nonviolence (*Satyagraha*) rooted in Christian love. The leader was the Reverend Dr. Martin Luther King, Jr., a living symbol of the middle class goals for which many Negroes had nearly given up striving. The strategy was seen in the Montgomery bus boycott, which gave Negroes all over America the image of *people* (not an organization or a court decision) with whom to identify in their aspirations. More important from a sociologist's point of view was the "breakthrough" of nonviolence into Negro consciousness as a way of thinking and acting for the long-floundering desegregation effort. Nonviolence was no longer a "mystical" practice of some disgruntled Hindus on the other side of the world. It was here and now, and in the deepest American South it worked.

The seeds for a full-fledged social movement were thus planted in a local movement, which reached its limited goals and soon took on the institutional form of the Montgomery Improvement Association. From 1956 to 1960 similar Improvement Associations were organized in other southern cities, and still other cities witnessed scattered "direct action" protests like that begun by the Negro lady in Montgomery who refused to give up her bus seat to a white man.

1960 on—"The Movement" (as everyone familiar with civil rights in America now calls it) formally began in February, 1960, when lunch counter sit-ins spread over the entire South in a few weeks. Four Negro students in Greensboro, North Carolina, had started it by confronting an everyday symbol of discrimination and inconvenience—the lunch counter at a "5-and-10-cent" store. The goal again was simple and easily understandable: sitting-down service at a lunch counter. The technique was equally simple and direct: sit down until served, ejected, or arrested.

By the end of the school year in June, 1960, there had been nonviolent direct action demonstrations against segregation in some 80 cities in the South, including every city of more than 100,000. Thousands of persons in the North and West picketed stores in more than 100 cities. Less than two months after the movement was triggered, the NAACP had no alternative but to broaden its official approach, and on March 17, 1960, its leaders called for a nationwide boycott of discriminatory chain stores and instigated sympathy demonstrations in many parts of the country.[19]

Successes came rapidly in the first summer, as city after city dropped barriers to equal service at lunch counters. And by early 1964, the scorecard looked something like this:

1. Desegregation of thousands of facilities (including lunch counters, laundromats, theatres, hotels) in approximately 200 southern cities.

2. Formation of over 50 biracial committees where no form of official communication between Negroes and whites had existed before.

3. Participation in direct action by several hundred thousand persons, Negro and white, North and South.

4. Arrests of 15,000 to 20,000 demonstrators.

5. An Interstate Commerce Commission ruling, resulting from the 1961 Freedom Rides, to enforce equal treatment in interstate transportation terminals.

6. Establishment of numerous voter education projects, resulting in thousands of newly registered voters in the South.

7. A radical change in Negro-white relationships all over the United States, including the growth of more militant Negro leadership, the birth of new civil rights organizations and revitalization of others already existing, intense direct action protest against many forms of discrimination by various levels of the Negro community, and the confrontation of the movement and the nation's political leaders which culminated in a broad civil rights bill being placed before Congress.[20]

THE MOVEMENT BECOMES A PROGRAM

The direct action movement against segregation differed from previous movements seeking Negro rights

[19] Individual NAACP chapters and members earlier had participated in direct action under their own initiative.

[20] Similar legislation subsequently passed, 1965.

in its spontaneity, its unpredictability, and its lack of coordination—in short, its charisma. But since February,
1960, there has been constant tension and interplay between spontaneity and institutionalization, as the attempt to organize a "good thing" has beset the sit-ins.
What began as an uncontrolled, spontaneous, rapidly
spreading movement in the 1960's was soon virtually
taken over by various organizations as a *program*. This
seems to be the fate of many spontaneous movements in
America today, where agency professionals and special-
ists in every field, with sophisticated mass media fund-
raising drives, and the proliferating organizations, are
waiting to take over and structure and merchandise social phenomena.

Social movements within highly differentiated societies tend toward much more rapid internal formalization
than in less complex social structures. This is so for at
least three reasons: (a) the highly rationalized organizational structures already existing readily absorb the
initial charisma, (b) mass communications technology
aids the rapid geographical spread of innovations, and
(c) ready-made ideologies already exist on a wider
level, and are more easily disseminated and reinforced
by a highly rationalized media system.

Herein lies the paradox of direct action: by definition
its purpose is to remain unbounded, to create unex-
pected crises, and to function as a charismatic catalyst in
a system of race relations where the dominant group repeatedly slips into lethargic paternalism. Just when both
the movement members and various opponents are feeling comfortable about predicting and to some degree
controlling the course of the movement, an Albany or a
Birmingham breaks out and upsets the best of strategists. So the urges for structure and nonstructure constantly pull at the heart of this movement. As a social
system, the movement drives toward what Max Weber
called *rationalization*—the tendency for social action to
differentiate into a system for attaining the commonly
agreed-upon goals of the actors by means of an increas-

ingly precise calculation of available and adequate means. But as individual human beings, the members oppose rationalization and bureaucratization. Direct action protestors do not read the rules of social movements, and would not follow them if they did, for a prime motive of nonviolent direct actors is to "beat" the system and the predictors, whether they be sociology and sociologists or Tradition and southern policemen!

THE FORMALIZATION PROCESS: MONEY AND MEMBERS

Formalization in the civil rights movement began almost before the first lunch counter stools were cold. There was an immediate need to organize for publicity, coordination of demonstrations, negotiation with businessmen and city officials—and, most pressing of all, for bail money and legal defense. Local movements, which had sprung up almost overnight in response to press reports and a sense of competition among Negro colleges, soon called on organizations like the Congress of Racial Equality (CORE), the Fellowship of Reconciliation (FOR), and the Southern Christian Leadership Conference (SCLC, the organizational extension of Dr. King) for guidance in nonviolent philosophy and techniques. Workshops and training sessions were being held in Greensboro and Nashville under the direction of CORE and FOR proffessionals within a week after the first sit-ins.

Within three months the movement had an organization of its own. Called together in Raleigh, North Carolina, at the urging of SCLC on Easter weekend, 1960, sit-inners from jails all over the South formed the Student Nonviolent Coordinating Committee (SNCC) to serve as a clearing house for information and coordination of diverse student direct action campaigns. Symbols of commitment and unity arose naturally from the situation: bandages from beatings and accounts of time spent in jail were prerequisite for high status. And this status-through-militancy system is in force in only slightly refined forms within the movement today. Competition in militance (whether jail-going or issuing of ultimatums to city officials or risking death trying to register voters in the Deepest of Deep South rural areas) has become the norm of success for SNCC workers as well as the older organizations.

Lapel buttons displaying black and white hands clasped together or simply an = sign are today becoming symbols which transcend the various organizations, but tension is still present between the civil rights groups involved in the movement. Early sources of strain were inherent in relationships between the student sit-inners and the adults who represented established civil rights groups, for this movement was from the beginning a revolt against authority of all kinds—custom, the NAACP, parents, Uncle Toms, Nervous Nellies, white policemen, pie-in-the sky Negro religion—in short, anyone or any institution not demanding immediate and total freedom from minority status based on color. The NAACP felt particularly threatened as people wondered aloud, and often, why the leading civil rights organization for nearly fifty years had not used this seemingly simple technique which brought so much desegregation so fast.

By June, 1960, the first year of the movement, the major organizations were meeting and issuing unity statements affirming their mutual respect and their public belief that "legal and educational approaches" are needed as well as direct action. But several times during 1961 and 1962 the movement was in danger of losing its thrust because of the organizational in-fighting: the NAACP was defensive, the students were aggressively critical of the "adult organizations" as they justified their own loosely organized (and highly effective) militancy, all the groups envied Dr. King's (and therefore SCLC's) fund-raising ability, and each proclaimed its own decisive role in desegregating the same facilities or cities. But motivated by the sheer weight of accumulated oppression, a small taste of freedom, and the eternal recalcitrance and occasional violence of many southern politicos and policemen, the direct action movement continued to grow, making strategic expansion into politics by registering voters in the Deep South.

One of the best indications of the metamorphosis from movement to established program is the growth rate of the three major direct action organizations: CORE, SCLC, and SNCC. CORE, the oldest of the organizations (1942), had a national staff of five and an annual budget of less than 50,000 dollars in 1959, the year before the sit-ins began. Within a year, the staff had increased to more than 15, and the budget to approximately 150,000 dollars. By 1963 the budget had grown to 775,000 dollars, and the number of national contributors had grown from 5,000 (in 1959) to more than 60,000.

SCLC, formed in 1957, did not increase greatly until 1960, growing from a staff of six and a budget of less than 100,000 dollars to a staff of more than 30 and a budget of between 750,000 to 1,000,000 dollars in 1963.

SNCC started in 1960 on a shoestring, and had only one full-time staff member and a mimeograph machine to keep students in remote areas of the country in touch with each other's activities, until the summer of 1961 when several students remade the organization. Voter registration (which was seen as a distinctly different kind of activity from direct action, but which *is* direct action amid the dogs, hoses, policemen, and church bombings of some Deep South areas) became an important SNCC program, and by mid-1962 there were 15 full-time staff members, some existing on as little as 20 dollars per week. But by the summer of 1963, SNCC was holding its own with a staff of 75 (including many field workers in rural Deep South voter registration) and an annual budget of 160,000 dollars.

Competition for funds and prestige continues, but the shock of a bombing or the assassination of an NAACP field worker has tended to cement relationships among the organizations, at least on the surface. Reintegration of fund-raising machinery was necessary in the face of excessive court costs, fines, and bail money if the movement-as-program were to survive. The March on Washington of August, 1963, brought together all the previously named civil rights groups plus the National Urban League, the National Federation of Negro Women's Clubs, and religious and labor groups in a massive one-day effort in which over 250,000 Negroes and whites showed a symbolic unity in the largest single protest demonstration in America's history. Organizational continuity was further assured when the NAACP, CORE, SCLC, SNCC, the Urban League, and the NFNWC later formed the Council on United Civil Rights Leadership in an attempt to pool fund-raising efforts for the desegregation movement.

In summary, the last decade in America has seen the thrust for desegregation turn into a full-blown social movement, with the initiative transferred from a relatively few professionals to a large number of militant individuals of every color and calling. The "leading Negroes" may no longer be the Negro leaders; the message-carriers of a decade ago have been replaced by militants who believe that they must stand up to The Man or lose followers to such separationist and supermilitant groups as the Black Muslims. Natural weaknesses in men and organizational egos have contributed to disunity, but the continuity of the movement has been maintained, as much by that nebulous sense of Soul built in to the situation of every Negro American as by any complex strategies. Bases of authority and appeal for money and members have been, in the long run, nearly as unstructured; they, too, are ready made in the character of anyone who has learned to want the goals of the American Dream, but who is denied institutional access to these goals because of his color.

A Negro sit-inner from North Carolina summed it up best—the prairie-fire spread of the movement, the high numbers of participants, the immediacy of success, the built-in legitimacy of goals and appeals and leaders. "It's like waiting for a bus, man. You know where you're going all the time, but you can't get there 'til the right vehicle comes along."

Chapter IV

METHODS OF
SOCIAL ACTION

Social action involves the efforts of a movement to change the ways of life of the people around them, to instigate reforms, to get laws passed, to sway or arouse public opinion, to win elections, to take command of social institutions, or in any manner to alter the structure or the functioning of the larger society outside the movement. Not all movements engage in this kind of social action. Some choose to develop their own ways of life in isolation from the larger society, either by withdrawing physically to a separate geographic area, as did the Mormons, or by setting up private partial existences in unobtrusive organizations which meet periodically, as do secret societies. In this chapter we are concerned with the ways in which a movement that does want to affect the whole society goes about doing so.

Techniques for instrumenting social action may be roughly divided into three categories: *violent methods, nonviolent methods, and quasiviolent methods.* Variations can be discerned and conditions under which one or another may be more effective can be described. We should note also that movements select techniques on grounds other than the rational criterion of efficiency.

Nonviolent Methods

To Americans the most obvious nonviolent method is to constitute *a voting majority*. The movement amasses members, tells them what candidates and issues to vote for, and "gets out the vote." The results are assessed when the votes are counted. However, except in gerrymandered political areas, it is rarely possible or feasible for a movement to control a vote exclusively through its own membership. In the first place, it is hard for a movement to get a majority of the voters to become members. Also, as was stated earlier, increased numbers often reduce consensus and control. Furthermore, attempting to win an election solely by votes of the organized members is inefficient because there may be many voters outside the movement who are sympathetic and still others who may be undecided and could be swayed long enough to cast a favorable vote even if they differ later on. Thus, the practical and more frequent technique is to *influence a voting majority*, which includes a great many nonmembers.

If the movement is well organized, it is easy to persuade its own members and there is little point in appealing to the determined opposition. Thus the logical target is the individual who because of conflicting pressures has no clear-cut personal interest in the candidates or the issues and may well not vote either way unless special pressures are brought to bear.

Although there may be little need to work directly on the members of the movement, an excellent indirect way of keeping them "in line" is to have them work on outsiders themselves. A man will usually sell himself more strongly on an idea when he tries to sell it to someone else. For example, if members can be put out into the field electioneering, their own interest sharpens, and their own vote becomes more secure. Arguments, facilities, and techniques vary in accomplishing this vote-getting. A movement with plenty of cars and willing

chauffeurs can expect more success than one which has
to try to convince the voter to walk four blocks to vote.
The basic principle is somehow to get the voter person-
ally involved in the election, even if he is voting merely
because the member-electioneer is such a personable fellow he hates to disappoint him. The more overlapping
reasons that can be mustered to involve him, the better
the chance that he will vote.

A third nonviolent method for accomplishing social
change is *obstructionism*. Where it is not possible for a
movement to have its own way, either by controlling or
influencing the vote, it may be possible to block the
efforts of its opponents. This is especially the case when
a large majority or plurality of the populace is required
for legitimate action. For years minority groups in
America and in France especially have employed this
tactic. It is condemned by some as a reflection of a "dog
in the manger" attitude, and certainly it is exasperating
to opponents, but in examining techniques of social action, moral judgments should not be confused with
judgments of efficiency. Obstructionist tactics are often
effective.

One technique of this sort identified with labor unions
is the strike. The more specialized the division of labor,
the easier it is for a small minority to stop the whole
works, as management and the public have learned
equally, often to their distress. In voting, where each
man counts for one, control of at least a third of the vote
is needed to block an opponent's plans. But in a production line, or any other highly interdependent structure, it
may be possible to obstruct action if merely one man
who is strategically placed is controlled. His productive
value may be slight, but his nuisance value may be enormous.

Some movements, notably extremist groups of both
"right" and "left," have gone to great lengths to place a
man at a strategic point in the system in case the time
would come when he could "throw a wrench into the
works." In war-time we call this sabotage, and at any-

time we are apt to scream loudly when someone does it
to us, but it is remarkably satisfying when we can do it
to the enemy.

The strike, which originally meant refusal to work
has many variations. Walkout strikes, in which the
workers leave the premises, are sometimes combatted by
substituting other workers or "scabs." Sit-downs block
this substitution, as do picket lines if they are respected.
Secessions of whole groups of officials or of participating
political units often need no picket lines because ther
are no possible substitutes. Thus, in the Korean War
when the North Koreans left the peace conferences
there could be no conferences at all. Devastating effect
may be achieved by a group in a position to give c
withhold effort, and obstructionist tactics must con
stantly be reckoned with by any group which can be s
opposed, even if they are not actually employed.

However, merely obstructing an opponent's plan c
action rarely achieves positive results; it is a defensiv
rather than an offensive gesture. In situations which pe
mit obstruction both parties usually need each other
support to get on with positive programs. Consequentl
obstruction is often only a temporary step to gain tim
for effective organization.

In cases where the movement itself cannot ma
enough power, a possible solution is to form a *coalitic*
with some other group. In this case, several persons (
organizations promise mutual aid and support, ofte
with considerable "log rolling" or bargaining for adva
tages. Such arrangements, however, are often hard
sell to members of a particular movement. Often coa
tions are reached only after each group demonstrates i
ability to obstruct the other if they try to operate sep
rately.

In short, several different kinds of problems and di
culties attend the formation of coalitions. First, leade
must find other groups with power to exchange. Th
they must design compromise programs in which ea
supports part of the other's plans in return for the su

ort he needs for his own. And the leader must judge
ow many of these side issues (some of which are only
·bitrarily related) his followers will accept without
eakening his control over his own movement.

While it might seem difficult to lead in such a situa-
on, it is often equally hard to follow, because faith and
edulity are often strained by the changing alliances.
We cited this in the discussion of the Communist Party
·llowers who could not accept the reasons for sudden
·ifts of the "line.")

For movements which are not cast in a political form,
· which deal with issues that are not decided politi-
·lly, the principal form of nonviolent action is persua-
on through mass media and personal contact. A move-
·ent in art or music grows not by "getting out the vote"
·it by persuading people to look and to listen. If pres-
ge figures, critics or celebrities in other fields lend their
·iblic support, this may attract many people, although
· t necessarily the most devoted.

Quasiviolent Methods

· step removed from nonviolent methods are certain
·iasiviolent methods which, while not actually violent
· themselves, depend for their effectiveness upon the
·ssibility of violence. These include the techniques of
·*reats* and *ultimatums*, whereby strong words raise in
·e minds of opponents the picture of violent actions
·hich will be taken if they do not comply with the
·ishes of the movement. International diplomacy uses
·is approach, as do small children bickering with their
·eighbors. The success or failure of this method depends
·eatly upon the picture which can be called to an op-
·nent's mind. If he is timid and imaginative, thinly
·iled threats stated in ambiguous terms may lead him
· imagine catastrophes far worse in many cases than
·e movement can actually produce. Less imaginative
·ponents may need to have the exact nature of the

threat spelled out for them. This poses a problem, however, because fears which are directly focused on specific dangers often lead to effective organization of resources in defense. If the danger is clear-cut and the opponent is powerless to oppose it, he may be intimidated, but if he too is powerful, it may merely inform him how best to defend himself. As in poker playing, a good bluff is hard to make, and some genuine show of power is usually necessary from time to time to sustain belief, lest the threats become the empty cry of "Wolf! Wolf!"

Early in 1965 this tactic was employed in Vietnam by both the Viet Cong and the Government forces, each trying by small scale military displays to convince the other that the potential "escalated" war was too costly to pursue, and thus to induce the other to retreat. Recently some of the southern Negroes have modified the nonviolent approach to form resistance movements such as the "Deacons" who make it known that they are armed and prepared for defense. The Ku Klux Klan has generally been credited with trying to control the Negroes and their white sympathizers by threats of violence. In all these cases, when the bluff is called, violence erupts.

Violent Methods

Violent methods of influencing social action include *riots, mass demonstrations, revolution* or *civil war, assassination,* and *terrorism.* In order to initiate violent actions, it is often necessary to *agitate* the population intensely. Accordingly, we may properly preface an examination of violent methods by a brief consideration of *agitation.*

Agitation does not always lead to violent action, although the two are often closely related. Agitation may be used merely to arouse public opinion in order to obstruct some present aspiration of the opponent, or to prepare the public to accept some new proposal, but prolonged, its ultimate outcome is apt to be violence. Some men find agitation so congenial and profitable that they become professional agitators, working for first one cause and then another. If he is a good craftsman and has no scruples, an agitator can usually find employment. For an able description of the characteristics of the agitator and his methods, see Lowenthal and Guterman's *Prophets of Deceit*.[1]

The leader of a social movement which seeks its goals through violence must frequently take the role of agitator, but few agitators demonstrate the other kinds of competence necessary to organize and maintain a social movement, with the result that frequently they play supporting roles in the movement rather than the dominant one.

Lowenthal and Guterman in examining the speeches and writings of leading agitators in the United States—Court Asher, Father Coughlin, William Dudley Pelley, and Gerald L. K. Smith—constructed a composite representing the typical "soap-box speech" of an agitator, in this case an anti-Semitic agitator.

THE AGITATOR SPEAKS [2]

When will the plain, ordinary, sincere, sheeplike people of America awaken to the fact that their common affairs are being arranged and run for them by aliens, Communists, crackpots, refugees, renegades, Socialists, termites, and traitors? . . .

Oh, this is a clever scheme and if the American people don't get busy and fight it the whole vicious thing will be slipped over on you without your knowing what hit you. A comprehensive and carefully planned conspiracy, directed by a powerfully organized clique, . . . is the ever lurking

[1] Leo Lowenthal and Norbert Guterman, *Prophets of Deceit*, New York: Harper & Brothers, 1949.

[2] "The Agitator Speaks" from *Prophets of Deceit* by Leo Lowenthal and Norbert Guterman. Copyright 1949 by the American Jewish Committee. Reprinted with the permission of Harper & Row, Publishers.

enemy of the people's liberty. Remember at all times that
the tactics employed . . . will be to create horror and panic
by exhibitions of maximum brutalities. . . .

Hitler and Hitlerism are the creatures of Jewry and Judaism. The merciless programs of abuse which certain Jews
and their satellites work upon people who are not in full
agreement with them create terrible reactions. . . .

Remember, these Jews expect to show no mercy to Christians. What is to prevent Jewish gangsters from doing damage to synagogues on purpose so as to create apparent
justification for retaliation—in which Christian Americans,
who know too much and have displayed too much courage,
would be picked up dead in or near synagogues?

We know what the stuffed shirts and reactionaries will
say. They will say we are crackpots. They will say that this
program will appeal only to the lunatic fringe. But surely
it is not anti-Semitism to seek the truth. Or is it?

What's wrong? I'll tell you what is wrong. We have
robbed man of his liberty. We have imprisoned him behind
the iron bars of bureaucratic persecution. . . .

While we have dissipated and persecuted management,
we have stood idly by and watched a gang of racketeers,
radicals, and conspirators regiment our workers in the name
of organized labor into a dues-paying conspiracy designed
in Moscow to recruit workers for what they hope would
become the American Red Revolution.

We are going to take this government out of the hands
of these city-slickers and give it back to the people that still
believe that 2 and 2 is 4, that God is in his heaven and the
Bible is the Word. Down must come those who live in lux-
ury, the laws that have protected the favored few, and those
politicians who are disloyal to the voters! . . . "Liberalism"
is destructive of all fundamental values. In matters pertain-
ing to Religion, Liberalism leads to Atheism. In Morals, it
leads to Nudism. In Politics, it leads to Anarchy. . . .

Alien-minded plutocrats roll in wealth, bathe in liquor,
surround themselves with the seduced daughters of America,
and cooperate in all schemes to build up pro-Communist and
anti-Christian sentiment. America, the vain—America, the

proud—America, the nation of gluttons and spenders and drinkers. When Harry Hopkins got married, Mr. Baruch arranged the party. There were seven kinds of meat served —twenty-two kinds of food, and it had cost Barney Baruch $122 a plate; and they drank of the vintage of '26. You talk about the drunken orgies of history—we expect Capone to live like that, but as long as I am a Christian soul, I will not be governed by a man like that. . . .

We leaders are risking our lives to write a new page in American history. We propose . . . to emasculate the debauchers within the social body and reestablish America on a basis where this spoliation can never again be repeated. I am attempting to speak one hundred times between the sixth of August and the fifteenth of September. This would be physically impossible for most men but thanks to the temperate and Christian life of my mother and father, I have been given a strong body and strong constitution. Even so, there will be nights that I will drop to the bed almost like a dead man, I will be so fatigued and exhausted. But I'll never throw mud at my opponent. I am led by the ethics and morals of Christ.

We are coming to the crossroads where we must decide whether we are going to preserve law and order and decency or whether we are going to be sold down the river to these Red traitors who are undermining America.

This meeting is not a lecture course, it is not an open forum. . . . we are making history here today. This is a crusade. I don't know how we can carry on without money. All we want is money from enthusiastic friends.

As Lowenthal and Guterman observe, agitators typically present a wide range of grievances against society and its leaders, including moral depravity, economic extortion, political perversion, and general cultural decadence. This is not so much intended to make clear sense to the listener as to capture his imagination and arouse bitter emotions, to generate "free-floating hostility" later to be directed by the movement. No real blame is placed on the listener, except to suggest that he has been a dupe and a sucker. Rather he is led to project. As one agitator puts it, "While we were praying they had their hands in our pockets."

The listener is pictured as an honest man in a hostile world. Everybody else is against him, everybody has an angle, a racket, and he has been too decent, too law abiding, too kind and trusting of his fellow man. The whole world is going to Hell and dragging him with it.

The enemy is a vague and sinister coalition of Wall Street Plutocrats, Washington Bureaucrats, Communists, Foreigners, Jews, Catholics, Labor Racketeers, and just about anyone who is not represented in the immediate audience and who is not directly known by the individual listener. This enemy is utterly without scruple.

On the other hand, the enemy has weaknesses. (Here the speech takes on the characteristics of a good Grade B Western!) The enemy is basically a coward, and would run if he met determined resistance. He is outside the law, but if the law can only be aroused from its lethargy, he can be apprehended. (Remember the sleepy sheriff in the Westerns?) But there isn't time to wake up the law—it moves too slowly. In this time of crisis, vigilante justice is the only cure. We have waited too long already, further delay may cost us our very lives. Following the Western analogy, it is at this point that we form a posse.

Riots. Even a skilled agitator cannot manufacture a riot completely at will, although he may be able to transform some crowds into mobs. The history of this kind of incited riot typically finds a large number of people who are already genuinely disturbed about some issue but who have not organized or planned any specific corrective action. In some cases a crowd may simply gather informally and unannounced, seeking information. The agitator and his associates mix with the crowd and talk, both in order to sense the feeling of the crowd and to plant their desired points of view. Anonymity permits license, and inflammatory statements

ay lead to a process of circular stimulation in which
ich man in the crowd is egging his neighbor on to do
mething.

Resentments are the raw material of violent action,
it first they must be intensified and focused. In trying
focus the resentment of a crowd and produce imme-
iate action the agitator may be inadvertently helped by
ightened authorities who over-react, such as "trigger
appy" policemen. Sometimes throwing one rock at just
ie right time can set the riot in motion.

Yet while riots incited on fortuitous occasions are use-
il to some movements, they do not usually form a com-
ete program. Prolonged violence requires planning
id organization, and may reach the point where a pri-
ite army, "goon squads," or "street fighters" engage
 stematically in skirmishes with the public and the au-
iorities. (Both Nazis and Communists did so in the
)20's in Germany and various movements are similarly
igaged now in Africa, Central and South America, and
ie Far East.) "Riots" planned out ahead-of-time some-
mes merge into guerilla war.

Demonstrations. A favorite form of *demonstration*
 the mass march, preferably to some shrine or seat
: government. Demonstrations are not necessarily
lanned to be violent, but at times become so, as can be
:en in the following example. In the United States in
394 "poverty armies" composed of jobless men planned
 march on Washington, a movement that "General"
icob S. Coxey called a "petition in boots." [3] The ac-
)unts of these adventures differ widely, and apparently
) did the adventures. Many of the men were tramps,
igrants, and soldiers of fortune. Others, perhaps most,
 ere merely semiskilled workers who could not find
 bs. In each case, a few self-appointed leaders with
)me flair for expression, a messianic zeal, or a rudimen-
 iry knowledge of military organization gathered a shift-
 ig following and lived off luck, the sympathies of the

[3] Donald L. McMurray, *Coxey's Army*, Boston: Little, Brown
 d Company, 1929.

populace, and occasional illegal appropriation of wha
ever was useful and loose. Sometimes, this "approp
ation" did not need to be loose. Much of the troub
between the armies and the law centered around the
predilection for riding trains without buying tickets.
some cases the jobless men "borrowed" entire train
which led to clashes with sheriffs, rangers, Pinkertor
detectives, and representatives of the railroads.

In hard times, however, Americans often sympathi
with the "little man" and many did so in these case
with the result that the armies proceeded moderate
well so long as they kept moving. Most communiti
seemed willing to donate food and clothing, buy a fe
radical books, listen to tales, for a day or two. But
every case where the army overstayed its welcome, fri
tion developed, which in some instances reached tl
proportion of riots. The technique of the "petition
boots" was firmly established in the American etho
however, as was the term "Coxey's Army," which b
came the symbol, not of the "Commonwealth of Chris
as Coxey had planned, but rather of a disreputable, c
sheveled, and disorganized mob, incapable of cor
manding respect or promoting effective action.

In later depression periods, others would march c
Washington, with varying results. Many World War
veterans recall with bitterness how in the 1930's Dougla
MacArthur, not yet a famous general, helped drive the:
off the government grounds. Yet in Washington, in 196
petitioners for Negro rights led a highly orderly marc.
Apparently the spirit of General Coxey, like that of Jol
Brown, goes marching on.

As the earlier quotation from Bob Darke notes, son
movements stage demonstrations in such a way as to a
tract "persecution" by the government and produ
martyrs for the cause. This clouds the line between vic
lent and nonviolent methods, since the aggressor is us
ally defined as the man who struck the first blow. (Se
regationists sharply question whether Reverend Marti
Luther King should have received a *peace* prize, claim

ıg that his actions precipitated violence, even though
ıe did not physically attack anyone.) In large demon-
rations it is rather easy for either side to plant *agents
rovocateurs* who officially start the fight in the name of
ıe other side and thus permit morally acceptable "de-
ınse" measures. In the resulting clashes it is very hard
ɔr the historian or sociologist to determine who, if any-
ıe, is telling the truth.

Broad-scale programs of demonstration, leading to
lanned and organized violence merge into civil war or
ıvolution. These events are characteristic of many
ıall, unstable societies in the Western Hemisphere and
lsewhere.

Revolutions. Long-term programs of violence aimed
t the overthrow of the existing government are usually
alled *revolutions,* although the term has been broad-
ıed by some writers to include overthrow of govern-
ıent by relatively nonviolent means, and I have used
ıe term earlier to refer to policies aimed at totally sup-
lanting some existing order. "Palace revolutions" or
oups d'état, in which persons already highly placed in
he system depose the leader and seize power them-
ɪlves, differ in numerous and rather obvious ways from
opular revolutions, which spring from less powerful
ɪople and which conform more closely to our outline of
ɔcial movements. It is often stressed that revolutions,
ke accidents, don't just happen. There are discernible
ntecedents, salient catalyzing crises, and at least the
ɪmblance of a regular pattern. The Old Regimes which
re later overthrown show distinct weaknesses in their
ɪconomic and political structure. Despotism is common,
s is inefficiency. The inefficiency may, in fact, be more
ɪpparent to the subjects than the despotism. But al-
hough privations exist, these obviously are not a suffi-
ɪient cause in themselves for revolutions, otherwise
ɔmeone would always be revolting.

The sociologist Lyford P. Edwards, in an early work
ɪn the subject, argues that one of the clearest symptoms
ɔf impending revolution is the "transfer of the allegiance

of the intellectuals" from support of the social system to attack on it.[4] Edwards sees the special function of the publicist as destroying the faith of the ruling class in their own legitimate authority, and adds: "A ruling class can survive even though it knows itself to be tyrannical. It cannot survive if it is made to appear foolish in its own sight."[5] This may be an overstatement, but most people do indeed need ideological support for their actions.[6] Crane Brinton pursues the same line of argument, and supports it with evidence from four major revolutions.[7] As general belief in the system falters, sporadic attacks begin.

In the four revolutions—English, American, French and Russian—Brinton found that the first clear action of revolt was protest and organized effort against certain taxes. This does not establish a necessary event in the pattern, but it does mark a plausible place for revolution to begin. If a few people get together and defy the government to collect money, they invite punishment on themselves, or they demand capitulation by the established authority. Either way, this gambit forces the government to make the next move. If it gives in, more demands and refusals will undoubtedly follow. If it prosecutes, the few protestors may become martyrs and incite more resentment among the masses, or they may escape and provide a legend of personal heroism and self-righteous courage, inspiring others to join them. Either way, the government is now on the spot.

Once the battle lines are drawn, and two clear alternatives presented, there is no room for the man who prefers to remain in between. At this point historical accounts diverge, the "Loyalist" historians claiming that

[4] Lyford P. Edwards, *The Natural History of Revolution*, Chicago: The University of Chicago Press, 1927, p. 38.

[5] *Ibid.*, pp. 63-64.

[6] For my own views along this line, see William Bruce Cameron, *Informal Sociology*, New York: Random House SS 21, 1963, pp. 133-153.

[7] Crane Brinton, *The Anatomy of Revolution*, New York: W. W. Norton and Company, 1938.

the revolution was accomplished by nefarious, though clever, schemers and charlatans, and the "Revolutionary" historians maintaining that there was a spontaneous "national" revival of honor and decency in the common man and that he forged ahead into violence with a fine religious fervor determined to cleanse the temple of money-changers and to sweep the tyrants from the throne. The truth, here as in many controversies, probably lies trampled somewhere in between. As Brinton says:

Actually, we must reject both extremes, for they are nonsense, and hold that revolutions do grow from seeds sown by men who want change, and that these men do a lot of skillful gardening; but that the gardeners are not working against Nature, but rather in soil and in a climate propitious to their work; and that the final fruits represent a collaboration between men and Nature.[8]

Using the four revolutions as basic data, Brinton develops a "model" of revolutions which is not exemplified completely by specific revolutions but which provides a general pattern descriptive of the way revolutions tend to develop.

At the point where the revolutionists resort to illegal acts of violence, the authorities step in and try to suppress them. Often the revolt dies at this point. But when the initial push is successful, a curious development is likely to follow—the "rule of the moderates"—a development which deserves some discussion.

Successful revolutions usually include a great variety of people, ranging from disenchanted intellectuals to seasoned professional politicians and military men, through all kinds of businessmen and workers, down to vagrants, hoodlums, soldiers of fortune, and barroom brawlers. If the revolutionists are overly prepared for resistance from the established authorities, the revolt appears to be a "pushover," and a new order is quickly established.

[8] *Ibid.*, p. 105.

The new order usually concerns itself with reforms: modifying the tax schedule, cleaning out graft and corruption in the courts, changing the method of promotion in the bureaucracies of government and the army, and perhaps improving the schools. The people who take charge are swamped with myriad petty details and become engrossed in trying to make the new regime effective. A frequent weakness of these moderates is that they are too sensible and pedestrian, too realistic about the problems of governing a society, and they fail to remember the violent feelings which they so recently aroused in the masses. (Such occurred in the early stage of Castro's revolution in Cuba.)

There may then rise more violent men, less educated and less experienced in government, but more emotionally in tune with the lower echelon followers. The followers have been built up to expect a grand struggle, a cataclysm, a holocaust which would sweep away all vestiges of the old regime and institute a radically different social order. Now they see the government being operated from the same buildings as before, with many of the same symbols and rituals, but a different set of men.

For the revolutionary extremists, this frustration is doubly bitter, because they haven't even won the fight. The moderates have. The extremists begin to resent the very peace which follows, and they suspect that anyone who achieves power is as corrupt as the previous rulers. The extremists feel cheated. The revolution is neither as "big" nor as exciting as they had expected it to be.

Couple these psychological events with the fact that the government does not suddenly become smooth and efficient, but rather plods along and stumbles, and we have real bases for discontent and the material with which the extremists can now agitate against the moderates. In the second act of this melodrama, the situation rapidly worsens. The extremists form cliques, clubs, private armies, and the like, many of which are used and supported by the moderates both as an attempt to conciliate them and also because organization is at a premium and almost any organized force is potentially useful. As tension mounts, subdued struggles ensue between the moderate and extreme forces over many petty issues, each adding to the bitterness and widening the cleavage.

The end of this struggle comes quickly when the extremists become fed up with trying to do business with the new bureaucrats and traitors (as they see them) and engineer a *coup d'état*.

The government which follows is a rough and tough dictatorship. It may be dignified under the title of "martial law," but in fact the military which rules is a new and an illegal government. And having thrown away the sanctions of legality which the moderates strove so hard to retain, the lid is thrown wide on Pandora's box and every kind of violence, terror, and malicious whim flies out. At this point the "reign of terror" may ensue.

The reign of terror is not necessarily, or perhaps even often, a planned program of excesses directed by the leaders. More often it is a widespread explosion of the sort which on a smaller scale is called a "riot." Suddenly a great many people find themselves involved. Violent actions against persons and property accelerate and much of the violence seems like a senseless, wanton attack on anyone or anything that makes a convenient target. In this situation the ordinary controls of law and order break down and any kind of frustration may be expressed in aggression, socially sanctioned by the surrounding mob if not the general society. Windows are smashed, automobiles upset and burned, strangers beaten, stores looted and destroyed as the mob exults in its new-found expression of pent-up hate.

Although Brinton's model presumes that the revolution was quickly accomplished by military methods, to be followed by a "honeymoon" which was later followed by the terror,[9] these phases may be observed separately and also in more peaceful revolutions as well.

The Civil Rights movement in the United States in

9 Brinton, *op. cit.,* p. 111.

recent years has been called an evolution by some and a revolution by others. Even some of the people who were willing to refer to the "Negro revolution" have thought that it could avoid violence, or at least that it could maintain a posture of defense and not be the initiator of violence. Most liberals have earnestly hoped and prayed that this would be true. Conservatives, and some hard-headed liberals as well, have pointed out that it is hard to suspend respect for law for a season, or to apply disrespect to only a few laws. A nonviolent revolution may be as anti-legal as a violent one, and the one may become transformed into the other. Although a philosopher may discern differences among laws and legitimize respect for some and disrespect for others, the average man is not this subtle, and if it appears to him that the force which supports law has broken down he is likely to violate any law he chooses.

In the light of our own recent history we may properly interpolate into Brinton's model a note about the violence in the Negro ghettoes in 1965.

As can be seen in the history of numerous uprisings, insurrections, or revolutions, the greatest violence does not necessarily occur when the fortunes of the revolutionists are at the worst. Very often violence takes place after there has been a significant but incomplete improvement in their condition. One might hypothesize that the improvement has kindled hopes which soar in proportion to the previous condition of depression and when these hopes are openly espoused and discussed they assume utopian dimensions which exceed the immediate possibilities. When the realization of the limitations sets in, and most people are not greatly better off than they were, two psychological events follow. The first is the bitter realization that the improved opportunities demand qualifications which they do not possess. (If, for example, the legal requirement to live in a ghetto is abolished, but it takes money to buy property outside, the poor man is still unable to move.) The second event is a reaction to the first, projection of guilt onto the "establishment" which has brought or accepted the changes. Leaders are charged with duplicity, the reforms are labeled fraudulent, and the whole scheme is seen as a deliberate attempt to ridicule the disenfranchised people. Once this mood is set, any pressure from the authorities may bring a violent explosion against the government which outsiders may regard as spontaneous, although, if we follow the above line of reasoning, it is not.

This kind of second wave of change is described by Lyford Edwards, Brinton and others and is a likely, but not essential phase in the pattern. This seems to be the basis for the Reign of Terror in Los Angeles which began August 11, 1965. Negroes who had long smoldered over poverty, disrespect, and general lack of success in a time of general prosperity and improving civil rights were suddenly caught up in a mass assault on the persons and symbols of white superiority. The initiating incident was the arrest of a purported drunken driver. The opening violence was directed immediately at the police. When this was not immediately suppressed, the riot spread and changed to a pattern of looting stores, vandalism against the offending property, and finally widespread arson. Looting provided weapons which led to sniping attacks on police and firemen and two days later something near to guerilla warfare with the national guard. Although hopelessly outnumbered and initially both planless and leaderless this mob did perhaps two hundred million dollars damage, threw an entire metropolis into a state of terror and carved a niche in history the precise meanings of which may be debated for a hundred years.

Although the Los Angeles terror developed during a relatively peaceful and non-military revolution, it fits much of the pattern Brinton and others have described. In a thousand and one minor details the "terror" proceeds. This is not the glamorous heroic of a Hollywood production; this is the nasty, petty annoyance suddenly engulfing the average man, which bears in addition the threat of sporadic eruption into a maiming murdering onslaught if he resists the new authority or is too slow in obeying orders. Politics suddenly becomes real.

In the model, the terror is a phase which accompanies the rule of the extremists. Usually they do not rule well. They have learned how to lead a ragtag army, they are good at breaking windows and horsewhipping traitors, but when it comes to running a whole country—including the vast majority of people, who do not normally engage in politics of any sort but try to make a living for themselves and their families and get along peaceably in the community—they do not have the needed expertise. Conflicts within and without the ranks are settled with summary violence. It is here that Thomas Hobbes' description of a "war of all against all" applies, and many a life becomes "nasty, brutish, and short!"

The economic distress which began to be felt under the moderate regime increases. Since the country has no stable government, local capital runs for cover and outside capital disappears. The average man now spends so much time in political concerns, listening to speeches, searching for information, whispering rumors, frantically trying to make sense out of the situation and to secure a safe place for himself in it, that his business goes to pot. The life of the full-time politician, trying to stay at the head of the avalanche, is even more hectic.

This frantic pace cannot last. It begins to burn itself out and people start pondering the effects of their own shocking behavior. The grand revolution looks tarnished. The Roman Holiday has left behind it a hangover. Stern military discipline and severe privation seem pointless. After all, what was the revolution for in the first place? People want to put life back together.

And so the reign of terror, or of virtue, depending upon one's position in it, passes. The dance halls reopen. Women dress up in pretty clothes. People start to give parties. Everyone tries to forget and have a little fun out of life.

Politically, the pendulum has completed its swing—slightly to the left, then far to the left, and now back nearer to center. If the church was banned, it may now be restored. Prisoners are granted amnesty. A few may even return to responsible positions. An attempt is made to redeem the government bonds. National debts may be paid. Diplomatic overtures are extended to foreign powers. An air of cheerful respectability replaces the fanatic countenance of terror. Back to work, repainting the store, replacing the shrubbery in the front yard, cleaning up the private and public mess. A new normalcy. The revolution has been accomplished.

In capsule form, this is the model of revolutions as seen by Brinton. This is not what always happens, as he freely admits, but if the events run full course this does seem a likely pattern.

Activism: permanent revolution. From knowledge of their own revolution Americans may be able to understand people who revolt in order to replace the government. They are less able to understand people who hate all government, all order, and who champion violent action as a continued way of life. The term sometimes applied to the ideology of continued violence is *activism* and one of the best literary presentations of this ideology is Georges Sorel, *Reflections on Violence*.[10]

Georges Sorel (1847-1922) was the chief spokesman of the radical syndicalist movement in France and had the utmost distaste for moderates of nearly any sort. He praises the kind of activism that is all engine and no brakes. From any standpoint, *Reflections on Violence* can hardly be called a "good" book. Badly organized and crudely written, its central thesis is antithetical to most of the tenets of middle class society. It is important because in its coarseness and immorality there is a glint of steel, a brief glimpse of the man of violence, the activist who hates reason and ritual and all the carefully bal-

[10] Georges Sorel, *Reflections on Violence,* New York: Peter Smith, 1941.

anced structures supporting middle class culture. He wants to smash through them as he slams his way toward the goal of a truth that lives in action alone.

For sheer sustained invective and bitterness this book has few equals. Sorel hates. He is the self-appointed spokesman for a mass of laboring men who have lost faith in the justice and even the workability of modern capitalistic society. Impotent in parliamentary government, bewildered by the complexities of economic organization, humiliated by the failure to wrest from the existing system the rewards they feel are rightfully theirs, as he sees it, their only recourse is raw violence. The fist on the jaw, the knee in the groin become high virtue.

Sorel respects nothing but force. Leaders, he believes, are automatically evil once they obtain power. They go soft, live easy, and prostitute the cause for personal gain. They become—and for him this is a very nasty word—politicians, which, curiously, is also a nasty word for the John Birch Society. Sorel curses intellectuals who try to think for the proletariat, without acknowledging this as his own self-chosen role. But an activist can dismiss logical consistency as a bourgeois fraud.

The brutal point of activism is this: the world does not have to make sense. Man does not have to think. Anything can be destroyed. The philosophy of action, if it can be called that, reduces itself to a frightening anarchy.

Young men who have not found a place in organized society and have no vested interest in the established order are especially susceptible, particularly if their formative years have been spent in the military or revolutionary forces. Viciousness and bravery which once served a legitimate goal persist, free-floating and restless. The "old soldier" finds himself untrained for quieter civilian pursuits, with no virtue but courage and no trade but violence. Taste buds burnt dull by fire can only be stimulated by more. The winds do not blow, the food lacks salt, and civilians do not salute. The war, once described as "damned dull, damned dirty, and damned dangerous," now is remembered in nostalgia as the only time he felt alive, and he is ripe for picking by some new and more violent leader.

Essentially this is what happened in Germany immediately following World War I, with the rise of the private armies, or *Freikorps*. The excuse for the organization of the *Freikorps* was that the struggling government of the Weimar Republic had inadequate police forces and volunteer civil guards were needed to protect the citizens against marauders, Communist revolutionaries, and common criminals. The psychological basis lay in the presence of a large number of young men who had been in the *Wandervogel* youth movements in their late adolescence, had fought in the War which they believed to have been lost only through the "stab in the back," and were neither emotionally nor technically equipped to re-enter civilian life. This was especially the case with many young officers, who had tasted power and prestige and did not want to give them up. Probably every war produces such a potential for private armies, but few countries have also had the political climate in which they could develop. An excellently documented and sobering description of this period is to be found in Robert G. L. Waite, *Vanguard of Nazism*.[11]

Later on, with Hitler's success, some of the activists left over from the free corps became heroized as his "old fighters," those who had been "at war with the enemy all the time." Ironically enough, some of these "old fighters," who were so useful to Hitler in the early days, became dangerous to him later when he consolidated his power and he ruthlessly sacrificed them. And indeed it is highly probable that had he not done so they would have devoured him, just as the extremists devoured the moderates in the French Revolution.

Closely related to revolutions is *assassination*. If the government concentrates power in a few key people, as

[11] Robert G. L. Waite, *Vanguard of Nazism*, Cambridge, Mass.: Harvard University Press, 1952.

in many authoritarian regimes, removing these people may effectively obstruct their policies, and may produce enough disorder for others to take over. Assassination frequently sets the stage for a palace revolution.

If the movement itself is weak, popular revolution is out of the question, but a single man may be able to assassinate another person, even if he pays with his own life in return. Not infrequently assassinations are arranged with this expectation in mind; one man is appointed, or selected by chance, to do the job without revealing the identity of any of his conspirators. He may even be prepared to commit suicide immediately thereafter to make sure the authorities will not capture him and force him to divulge information.

Beyond the immediately practical obstruction which is wreaked by assassinating the key man in an organization, the symbolic value of their violent deaths sometimes has a sobering and frightening effect on lesser men who might want to step into their shoes. If one ruler or leading official can fall, so can another. Having happened once, it can recur. When assassination is used repeatedly, it merges into terrorism.

Terrorism is a rather simple technique, and sometimes has what appears to be at least a temporary efficiency. Terrorism is closely related in its effect to obstructionist measures, but usually is applied by a movement which already has a fair amount of power, or expects to obtain it soon. The immediate objective of a systematic campaign of terror is to reduce the predictability among those being terrorized. If people can't predict, they worry and fear, and usually are led to expend their resources for counteraction. At the very least, it will cost them a great deal of time and effort to prepare defenses. And at the most it will vitiate any action they might otherwise take. How is this to be done?

Whereas attempts at assassination can be expected by most key figures in authority so that they can predict and guard against such a move, the terrorist program often seems to strike at random. For example, a top man who has caused considerable trouble for the terrorist movement may be killed—an understandable fact from the movement's viewpoint. This may be followed, however, by the murder, say by a bomb, of anonymous and "innocent" persons in the public market. A few days later, masked men dash into a hotel lobby and machine gun the first four people they see. The very randomness of the murders permits no plausible theory of priority— anyone might be next. If wanton violence is mixed with equal excesses of generosity, predictability at this point breaks down almost entirely, and the populace feels all at sea. Psychologists would say they face an unstructured situation. The scene around them shifts wildly and the familiar behavior of others from which they normally take their cues for response is lacking, or can't be trusted. They don't know what to think except that all kinds of unforeseen dangers may at any time await them. The situation resembles James Branch Cabell's description of Walpurgis Eve "when almost anything is rather more than likely to happen." Bombs are a preferred tool of terrorists, and have been used in recent years by the Algerians in France, segregationists in Alabama, the Viet Cong in Saigon, and various groups in Africa.

Terrorism has also been used by totalitarian groups to shatter the morale of a specific individual. A familiar and frequently reported pattern is about as follows: First he is seized in the middle of the night and taken to a strange place where he is beaten and thrown into a cell. After treatment so harsh that he may be ready to give up all hope and die, he is removed, given a bath, clean clothes, and a good meal—with the deference and respect which befitted his former status, and he is politely asked how he is getting along by persons seemingly unaware of his recent mistreatment. As his hope rises that he is dealing with reasonable men after all and he starts to mobilize his personality for the old familiar ways of behaving, he is subjected to even worse treatment than before. A few such alternations, each involving different elements from those he has met previously, and only a rare individual can summon the moral and mental powers to comport himself as a normal human being.

Books like *Bushido* and *Out of the Night* record individual responses to this kind of terroristic process, and Bruno Bettleheim and others have described prison camp situations in which similar destructive treatment was accorded whole groups of people, with varying results.[12] George Orwell's fictional description of the torture and ultimate collapse of the hero in *1984* gives insight into the psychological processes involved.

Terrorism can immobilize a population. Moving swiftly and unpredictably to keep the citizenry off balance, apprehensive, and disorganized, the terrorist movement can temporarily maintain a kind of control. The costs to the beleaguered population are great. The material costs alone are usually very large: production suffers, distribution is disrupted, and the economy may near collapse. If the terror is not swiftly consolidated into firm control, counteroffensives may arise, with fearful reprisals. Whether the terror campaign succeeds or not, the moral costs to the movement are often high, and may undermine the norms which previously provided the rationale for political control. This happened in Germany after the "Night of the Long Knives," in which Hitler purged the Old Fighters. Previously, whatever its infringement on the older social customs, the Nazi Party had operated through legal channels, at least in form. But after this terroristic action, the law could no longer be appealed to for prestige and sanction. In effect, a short term advantage was bought at the price of a much longer one, and one of considerable importance.

Once terrorism—or "lynch law" in the American

---

[12] Alexandre Pernikoff, *Bushido*, New York: Liveright Publishing Corporation, 1943. Jan Valtin (Richard Julius Herman Krebs), *Out of the Night*, New York: Alliance Book Corporation, 1941. Bruno Bettleheim, "Individual and Mass Behavior in Extreme Situations," in *Readings in Social Psychology*, S.P.S.S.I., New York: Henry Holt and Company, 1947, pp. 628-638.

phrase—becomes the precedent, anyone who is strong enough may employ it. For when the justification for the established order is gone it is largely power that remains. It is very dangerous to reduce social issues purely to power problems, however, because power, uncontrolled by legitimate authority, can be used for the advantage of the few at the expense of the many.

I have devoted considerable discussion to assassination and terror in relation to revolutions because they play an important role in world affairs today, but are phenomena with which most Americans have little direct experience. This emphasis should not be interpreted to imply that all revolutions are merely terroristic or proceed from bloodthirsty motives. Lyford Edwards,[13] in refuting this view, has claimed (as have many others) that economic incentives underly all successful revolutions, and argues that violence is only a means to an end. He brings considerable historical material to bear to show that systematic and deliberate terror can shortcut the process of change where rational methods would probably fail, producing beneficial social consequences. In other words, violence is a consciously bargained price, and a small one at that. In contrast, Pitirim A. Sorokin, who witnessed and was a victim of the Bolshevik takeover in Russia, sees in revolutions all manner of depravity and the antithesis of conscientious reason.[14] Many other writers have debated the pros and cons of revolutions.

Generalizations about the social, and individual, benefits and costs of revolutions are very difficult to support, and certainly cannot be treated adequately in this brief discussion of one complex type of social movement, of which there are many variations. At times, terror and atrocities go hand in hand with compassionate decencies and needed innovations. We do know that revolutionary periods, in which the whole social order is

[13] Lyford P. Edwards, *op. cit.*, p. 69 and pp. 156-185.
[14] Pitirim A. Sorokin, *The Sociology of Revolution,* Philadelphia: J. P. Lippincott Company, 1925.

challenged and upset, are often marked by what Emile Durkheim called *anomie*, or normlessness. In such times, guessing what others are likely to do next becomes more difficult than it ordinarily is, and that is usually difficult enough.

The bulk of the description in this chapter has been concerned with violent methods, partly because of their inherent drama, and partly because some of the nonviolent methods of persuasion and legislation are so familiar to most Americans that they hardly require extensive recounting. There are other nonviolent methods which have been employed for a long time but are not part of the everyday experience of most people, and which in some cases involve a rather sophisticated technique and an elaborate supporting ideology which is at variance with much of our ethos.

Although the basic ingredients of what is now called "nonviolent direct action" have been around for a long time—centuries in fact—their synthesis into a systematic workable program of great effectiveness and relative precision is largely credited to the late Indian leader, Mohandas K. (Mahatma) Gandhi.[15] The movement of Gandhi, and the techniques employed, are especially relevant to the current scene in America, because they provide the model for the Civil Rights movement as represented by such leaders as Martin Luther King. Gandhi was the first political leader to use the nonviolent approach on such a grand scale, with impressive results, culminating in the liberation of India from British rule.

[15] Although *Satyagraha* is the prototype of modern techniques of nonviolence, numerous variations occur. A discussion of the range is found in: Gene Sharp, "The Meanings of Non-violence: A Typology (revised)," *The Journal of Conflict Resolution*, III, No. 1, March, 1959, pp. 41-66.

An Example of Nonviolence: Satyagraha

For Americans who typically think in terms of action, the idea of passivity suggests impotence. Nonviolent coercion is to such persons a contradiction in terms. To understand how this method could arise, we must try to understand its background. The remarkable revolution led against the British by Mohandas K. Gandhi can be understood only when seen against the background of Eastern philosophy and religion, Eastern desires for autonomy, and the unbelievable poverty and scarcity which has marked Eastern economics ever since we can remember. India's chief problem is population—enormous masses of people divided by social and geographical differences. Almost anything which is too plentiful is cheap, including human life: in India as in much of the Orient, human life is not worth much, and certainly not valued as in America. Reincarnation in the "wheel of life" is, in this framework, not a divine promise but a diabolical threat, condemning a person to cut teeth and lose them, suffer diseases, undergo privations, and die and do it all over again until infinity. The passivity of Nirvana—an escape through renunciation of the body and the world, an escape into sheer nothingness—is approximated in our culture only in the hopes of people under extreme duress, such as soldiers who have fought to near exhaustion, or Negro slaves whose greatest hope was to lay down their burden.

A striking aspect of *Satyagraha* is the elaborate predictions which inhere in it. There is a note of fate, a kind of tragedy in which all is foretold, the good and the bad, move by move, with no trick surprises, but with a grinding deliberation. Gandhi told people what he intended to do, often somewhat apologetically, and then went ahead and did it. His predictions were very often correct.

The movement of nonviolence started in South Africa in 1906, when the Indian minority there was chafing under increasing governmental restrictions. At a public meeting of expatriate Indians discussing the new laws and demanding that "something should be done about it," Gandhi arose and announced that he intended to disobey the discriminatory ordinances and take the consequences, whatever they might be. His reputation as a successful lawyer and a man of principle gained him a hearing, and the fact that there was indeed no other proposal which appeared workable added to the determination of others to follow suit. Right then and there a social movement was born. In the press and elsewhere this disobedience was regarded as a weapon of the weak, and called "passive resistance." Gandhi rejected the term and coined the word *Satyagraha,* a Sanskrit compound combining "truth" with "force," which has been translated as "Soul Force" or "insistence on truth," for people who could not manage the un-Western sounds.

In this basic notion is a mixture of Christ's admonition to turn the other cheek, the expiation of guilt through suffering, Thoreau's proposals of civil disobedience, and perhaps a touch of masochism—Gandhi's previous behavior suggests that he felt a need for self-inflicted pain. In addition, there is a malice inherent in the plan, like that of the Scotsman who counseled his hot-tempered son, "Always give a man a soft answer in an argument; the Good Book says you should, and besides, it makes him madder than anything else you could say!"

To Westerners, the whole business of hurting one's self in order to influence others may seem like the tantrum of a spoiled child who holds his breath until his mother pleads with him to stop; the implication is that he is exploiting her love for him, and that if the love is not there, the device won't work. Also, there is the conviction that the child will not keep it up if he is not rewarded. Gandhi pushed this principle further. He was perfectly complacent in the face of repeated failure. If death is to come, it is to come. The fatalistic disregard for personal misfortune supported him where our spoiled child would likely quit.

The tradition of hunger strikes, "sitting dhurna," is well established in India. It has a curiously compelling effect, challenging the imagination and at the very least making the authorities nervous. The prediction in it ("If you do not do as I ask I will starve and you will be my murderer.") may be illogical, but it is impressive. So, too, with other cheek-turning procedures. Most dramatic is the result of the sitdown strikes in public squares. Police arrive and politely ask the strikers to move on. The strikers smile and refuse. The police threaten violence, the strikers again smile and refuse, the police repeat their threats, and the strikers say, "It would be a shame for you to do such a thing, but if you must, you must." So the police break a few skulls, cart some people off to the jail, and perhaps shoot some others. With what result? Those who remain still smile and say, "It's too bad that you people behave so crudely," and other people take the place of the fallen.

This method has been compared psychologically to jujitsu, in that it opposes strength with weakness and thereby throws the opponent off balance. Men, at least ordinary men who make up most police forces, cannot continue dealing out violence to people who offer no resistance. They get sick of it, their consciences trouble them, they develop an uneasy fear that they have run into something much bigger than themselves, and sometimes they even undergo a sort of religious conversion to the other side. Conceivably, a police force of pure sadists might enjoy such a situation, but there are rarely enough sadists available, and, besides, it does nothing except use up a lot of energy, destroy an infinitesimal part of the population, and give the authorities a very bad press. Authorities sometimes become confused, with the result that a victory is achieved for nonaggression.

The characteristic American reaction to this method is that "It simply wouldn't work here!" by which at least two things are meant. First, Americans wouldn't sit still and absorb violent attack; second, they are firmly convinced that if someone used this procedure, authorities would forcefully prevent it and subdue those who attempted nonviolence. Yet, this is not necessarily the case, as indicated by the following example.

This occurred in a conscientious objector's camp during World War II. The new commanding officer gathered the men together and gave them a hell-fire and brimstone lecture, insulting and inflaming them and obviously inviting a fight, which he was prepared to win. At the conclusion, he belligerently demanded, "Now, are there any questions?" In the group were several Quakers, one of whom rose and faced the gathering. "Friends," he said, "I think this is an appropriate time for a Silence." A "silence" for the Quaker has meanings far beyond the passive suggestion of not speaking—it includes contemplation, meditation, and other ideas of great spiritual meaning for him. In this case, however, the effect was that every man in the group simply sat and looked at the Major. The latter in turn, having whetted his appetite for a fight, tried to glower back, but succeeded only in chewing up two cigars and developing a bad case of the "shakes," no doubt complicated with the secret feeling that he had probably made a fool of himself. This may be one key to the technique for *Satyagraha* makes the opponent look, and feel, foolish.

The journalist and sociologist, Krishnalal Shridharani, in *War Without Violence*,[16] has abstracted the total plan of *Satyagraha* into about a dozen steps, including alternative procedures at certain points. These are paraphrased here.

1. The first step involves negotiations and arbitration, which are initiated for two principle reasons. First, they may get the desired results. If not (which is more

[16] Krishnalal Shridharani, *War Without Violence*, New York: Harcourt, Brace and Company, 1939. Paraphrased by permission of Mrs. Sundari K. Shridharani.

likely), they demonstrate the willingness of the movement's leaders to be polite and correct and their reluctance to take direct action. It is a kind of "bending over backwards" designed to leave no doubt in the mind of the public as to the high moral purpose of the movement.

2. Failing in negotiation, agitation is then undertaken to inform the public of the problems and keep the issues alive. This stimulates the morale of the members of the movement and disturbs the opponent's complacency.

3. When the public is sufficiently aroused, demonstrations are made and an ultimatum is issued stating minimum demands. One effective demonstration used by Gandhi was the *hartal*—a cessation of all activities, as in mourning. Other violations of normal procedure may also be used.

4. Self-purification intensifies the impression of the movement's morality. There is much public prayer and fasting. The leaders confess publicly that the terrible situation which has developed is in part their own fault and prescribe elaborate penances for themselves and their followers. These include abstaining from luxuries of all kinds, resigning lucrative government posts, and not using various commodities. In India this technique produced obvious suffering by the members, but it also undermined the financial and organizational position of the rulers because the things given up were heavily taxed and the positions from which they resigned could not readily be filled. In this way, members had the double satisfaction of being devout martyrs while stabbing their opponent where it hurt.

These first four moves comprise a major strategy which sets the stage for other kinds of action in which alternative procedures may occur, some tailored specifically to the agricultural, others to the industrial situation. The next three steps apply especially to industry.

5. The strike is used in the strategy of *Satyagraha* very much as it is used in Western countries, with the

specification that where possible an attempt is made to establish a general strike in all industries and service occupations in a given area.

6. Picketing is set up, principally as a means of demonstration and advertisement, gaining sympathy from the populace, and inviting persecution from the authorities.

7. The *Dhurna*, which has been called the "father of the sit-down strike," is a move designed to be effective even if it is suppressed. It is especially effective in industry because no firm which sells to the public can ignore a bad public opinion. The only way a *Dhurna* can be crushed is by violence and bloodshed. If the strikers resolutely refuse to fight back, violence toward them will anger the public. Shridharani recounts how some 30,000 men, women, and children sat down in a main street in Bombay when the police refused to let them continue their march. Matters seemed to be at a stalemate, and a rainstorm came up. Sympathetic citizens organized "relief corps" to provide food, water, blankets and other comforts for the strikers. The *Satyagrahis* in turn delivered these to the beseiged policemen as a gesture of love and goodwill. About midnight, the police simply gave up and let them continue their triumphant march. What else could they do with 30,000 "friendly people?

8. A severe blow at a colonial government is the economic boycott, in which the products of the ruling group are simply not used. This was a telling move in 193 when Gandhi boycotted imported cotton goods. By reducing his wearing apparel to a homespun loincloth, he threatened the clothing industry. For industries that export operate on a basis of extended credit, and transportation, insurance, warehousing, and import and export taxes are paid in effect before the goods are sold and any sudden downward shift in the retail market demand leaves the businessman with a large and unmanageable inventory which costs heavily every day that

it remains unsold. A total stoppage of sale in a normally large market area for only a few months could destroy many businesses. Traditionally, colonial expansion has served commercial interests. When commerce is thus threatened, colonial politics take on a different look.

9. More serious and less legal than the boycott was the nonpayment of taxes. This, in line with Thoreau's ideas, is a clear case of civil disobedience, and one which could be applied by rural and urban people alike. The immediate results in India were wholesale arrests, confiscations, and finally terrorism by the British, with the usual smiling acquiescence by the Indians. The long-run result was that after jails were filled, arrests became almost meaningless, and continued hounding of the nontaxpayers brought them sympathy. Confiscation was met with the next step, which logically follows, *Hizrat*, or mass exodus, in which a whole community simply packs up and leaves. The oppressive government, left with no population to govern, then may bargain to try to induce the people to return.

10. There follows a period of what (perhaps redundantly) is called "noncooperation." At this point Indians were urged by the movement to forego all government jobs, give up honorary titles, withdraw from the army and the schools, not use the courts to settle grievances, and in other ways make the existing government appear unused and useless. This tactic was enforced by social ostracism of all Britishers and of any Indians who still fraternized with them or tried to hold government jobs.

11. Next, direct conflict with the law is sought. At first, in the Indian revolution, certain manifestly unjust laws were broken, as a symbol of revolt, one of the most famous ones being Gandhi's "March to the Sea" to make salt from sea water in violation of the salt tax law. Such demonstrations stirred the imagination of Indian patriots. After sufficient publicity and sympathy had been aroused, laws were then broken indiscriminately, as a matter of principle. Here again, the authorities soon be-

came overwhelmed, because there are never enough policemen or enough jails to control people if they are determined to disobey.

12. Once the existing government has been embarrassed by its inability to cope with lawbreakers and by the unwillingness of citizens to use its resources in meeting their problems, there remains one last step—to take over governmental functions and set up a parallel and, ultimately, altogether new government. At this point, the coup is complete.

The complete plan of *Satyagraha* was never fully carried out because other historic events intervened. These are amply described in numerous books about India and about Gandhi himself. Here it should be emphasized that an elaborate plan of revolution was conceived in which the revolutionists abstained from doing direct bodily harm to the party in power.

It may be argued that this so-called peaceful movement was not at all peaceful, but merely subtly violent, since the movement did do serious damage to the British economy, unseated career people, and certainly incited violence on the part of others. However, the fact remains that so long as Gandhi's ideas were in control, the *Satyagrahis* themselves did not commit violent acts. To be sure, they did sacrifice their members to the violence of their opponents, but they do not appear to have lost more people than they probably would have lost in pitched battles had they attempted revolution by violent means. When we add to this reflection the fact that they had no other viable choice, being economically unable to train and equip armies, we are faced with a very sobering possibility—namely that "peaceful" means may in the long run be even more effective than violent ones. Having an army is no sure guarantee of power over people who have none.

Reflecting briefly on the pattern established by Gandhi, it becomes clear that this technique might be used by any large minority group which shared similar limitations and could accept the supporting philosophy. From the 1930's on astute observers predicted that American Negroes might use the technique and in recent years they have done so with increasing frequency and effect. As part of the current appeal is legitimized by Christian doctrines, and as the Civil Rights program simply seeks to make effective rights already supposedly guaranteed by law, the movement has received considerable support from white clergy of various faiths and from liberal college students.

It may be expected that nonviolent methods derived from those of Gandhi will continue to be employed by social movements, especially in the stable Western societies.

Chapter V

SOME QUESTIONS OF ASSESSMENT

In reflecting on the significance of social movements, at least three important questions remain. First, nearly every movement produces innovations and we need to explore their meaning. Second, an important question which has recently attracted renewed attention concerns the importance of emotional involvement in the search for meaning in life. And, third, beyond the importance of the movement in giving meaning and purpose to the lives of its members, what will it do for the rest of us? After a brief examination of these three questions, this chapter concludes by suggesting the requirements of a usable theory of social movements.

Special Techniques and Terminologies

For several reasons it is worth examining social movements for special techniques and terminologies. These provide some of the "color" of the movement, setting it apart from other movements and from the rest of society. Secondly, they may suggest other aspects of the movement, or help us understand aspects which seem

uperficially unrelated. Thirdly, the key to interlocking
movements is sometimes to be found in their similar
modus operandi, or else the similarity may result from
common underlying intellectual and other influences
where no actual collaboration exists. Finally, goals and
ends often masquerade as means; this is to say that peculiar procedures carried on by the movement and explained by them as expeditious responses to social exi-
gencies may instead be the genuine *raison d'être* of the
movement for some of the members.

The regalia and the names of officers sometimes suggest deep needs of members. As James W. Vander Zanden says:[1] "The elaborate Klan regalia conspicuously es-
tablishes the individual's membership in the 'Invisible
Empire' and sets him apart from the mass of humanity.
The concern with status and individual aggrandizement
is reflected in the organization's preoccupation with in-
signia, with the assignment of status-denoting colors for
the robes of officials, and with the use of an exaggerated
status-exalting nomenclature (e.g., Imperial Wizard,
Grand Dragon, Grand Titan, Grand Giant, and Exalted
Cyclops)."

The affinity of the Bop musicians for Mohammedanism was a unification of several diverse attitudes. They
were tired of the old jazz, and tired also of the old preju-
dices against Negroes. Since American Negroes are
traditionally Christian, Boppers generally rejected
Christianity. Mohammedanism is widespread in Africa;
by assertively identifying with African origins they repudiated white America. Moreover, while a Negro
might ordinarily be refused service in many places of
business, if he were wearing a turban he might be admitted, which was both a convenience and a satisfying
joke on the whites. Thus the religious conversions of the
Boppers were basically related to their music through
the common spirit of revolt against their local culture.

People who have studied the Communist movement

[1] James W. Vander Zanden, "The Klan Revival," *The American
Journal of Sociology,* LXV, March, 1960, 460.

carefully have learned to spot certain peculiarities of phraseology which most of us do not use. A simple example is the term "functionary" as a noun denoting a person who does a bureaucratically prescribed job in some kind of "apparatus." Common vocabularies do not necessarily mean common membership, but they bear further examination and explanation. Perhaps enemies who constantly scrutinize each other may come to share a language. The writer has found some typically Communist phraseology in publications of the John Birch society.

In addition to search for linguistic clues, the *modus operandi* approach may apply to techniques of demonstration, fund raising, propaganda publication, social control, and so on. Observing that a new movement acts in ways typical of some older one provides a hypothesis in unraveling its background and purposes.

As most social movements are dedicated to change, new terminologies mark almost every new movement, except when they try to symbolize their linkage with a past. Less frequent are new techniques of other sorts, but some interesting ones do appear, and if they seem to work they may be quickly copied.

The Jehovah's Witnesses were one of the first movements to make extensive use of phonograph records, and in a curious way. Missionaries from the group, when asked embarrassing questions, would not attempt to answer, but rather produce a recorded speech by Judge Rutherford and a portable record player. The critic could hardly interrupt the record, and if at its end he still pressed for an answer, he got another record. More commonly, recordings of speeches are used to recapture the spirit of some great event or recall the charisma of the leader. Used in this way, records have been released by various movements. For instance, Madalyn Murray purveyed a two-record album on "Why I Am An Atheist," and a popular item among liberals has been the inaugural address of the late President Kennedy. (One company pairs this with President Eisenhower on the other side.[2])

In 1964, a fund raising letter from the Council for a Livable World directed:

————If your last name begins with letters A - Ham contribute to the campaign fund of Senator Gale W. McGee.

————If your last name begins with letters Han - Rex contribute to the campaign fund of Senator Frank E. Moss.

————If your last name begins with letters Rey - Um contribute to the campaign fund of Congressman Joseph M. Montoya.

————If your last name begins with letters UN - Z contribute to the campaign fund of Congressman Ralph R. Harding.

Many "new" techniques are essentially variations on a theme. One old and frequently reworked theme is the "chain letter." One might think variations of this technique had been exhausted, but early in 1964 university teachers and professional men who were thought to sympathize with the civil rights movements received the following letter:

This concerns the death of Medgar Evers in Mississippi. There are several needs that follow his tragic shooting: (1) his family needs help; (2) a large group of Americans need to express their position on this matter; (3) we need to say something effective to the governor and the people of Mississippi.

An idea has been conceived by some of our friends that might accomplish these three purposes in one act. We propose to flood Governor Barnett's desk with envelopes containing checks for $1.00, which will automatically make him trustee of money that he can only deliver to the Evers family. An attorney says that the checks should be made out

[2] Spoken Arts SA 827.

exactly as follows: "Ross Barnett, Trustee of Memorial Fund of Family of Medgar Evers." They should be mailed to Governor Ross Barnett, State Capitol, Jackson, Mississippi.

A number of us are receiving and transmitting this proposal as a chain of human concern. I'm writing to nine other people whom I think as concerned as yourself. If you will write to ten persons who you think would be interested, and if the letter goes through five people in an unbroken chain, the Governor should receive 200,000 envelopes on his desk within ten days.

I hope this will interest you.

Sincerely yours,

In this example, civil rights sympathizers may find the *process* as appealing as the *product*. And, as in many situations requiring persuasion, the more appeals overlap the more they reinforce. Outsiders may criticize a movement whose members enjoy what they are doing as being hypocritical, but not all kinds of social change must be bought by martyrdom and self-sacrifice, and the possibility of enjoying one's activities while following the path of righteousness provides a very strong appeal indeed.

The end point in the confusion of means and ends is seen when a movement has clearly worked itself out of a job, but persists nonetheless and perhaps even searches for new jobs to do so it can keep going. This is more likely to be the case if the movement has already become institutionalized with an elaborate formal structure and a professional staff. Criticism based upon this kind of functional change has been leveled at the movement organized to find a cure for infantile paralysis which after the development of Sabin and Salk vaccines has found reasons to continue. In such cases, some people stand to profit from the method of operation regardless of the object. Emotionally, these professionals may be poles apart from the "true believers" who founded the movement or gave it support. Just as agitators may become specialized craftsmen purveying their services to various movements, so also may researchers, publicists, fund raisers, organizers, and others. Following the careers and work of such professionals might provide us with considerably more insight into social movements than we have today.

The whole question of leadership is complex and leads far beyond social movements. It may be argued that the only characteristic common to all leaders of social movements is that they have followers. The kinds of leadership and of followership seem related to other salient characteristics of particular movements and not subject to easy abstraction.

Studies of leadership take different directions.[3] Some analyze psychological traits of leaders, either behavioral mannerisms or underlying patterns of character structure. Others concentrate upon skills or techniques, often apart from the personal qualities of those utilizing them. Some describe social situations which permit or demand leadership. But while all of this is informative, it remains incomplete. It provides a vocabulary for discussion, typologies with which to classify observations, and techniques to test empirically. However, it would appear that many of these factors are interactive, and even a very standardized situation may permit great variation in technique of leadership, which in turn may reflect basic differences in personality.

Gunther Schuller once compared orchestral conductors, noting that while Toscanini succeeded by intimidating the players, Bruno Walter got results because the men liked him so much that it would be impolite to play poorly; they might hurt his feelings. The point could be elaborated with reference to baseball managers or others who lead in rather standardized situations. Leaders are those who somehow get people to follow them. Even Max Weber's analysis of charisma does not indicate what is unique about the leader; "charisma" simply

[3] See, e.g., C. Gibbs, "Leadership," in G. Lindzey, ed., *Handbook of Social Psychology*, Vol. II, Cambridge, Massachusetts: Addison-Wesley Press, 1954, pp. 877-920.

means that somehow leaders attract by their personal characteristics. They all do *something* exceedingly well. When they stop doing it well they often cease to lead.[4]

The Necessity of Engagement

Every philosophy which becomes popular leaves its mark on the vocabulary of a people, and illuminates their concerns by its own peculiar light. The recent interest in existentialism has made many people think about life in terms of engagement (or its opposite), confrontation, commitment, assertion, and so on. Although most existentialist philosophy is more sophisticated and intellectual than the activism of Sorel, nonetheless it emphasizes action, emotion, and involvement, all of which run somewhat counter to the tenets of positivism, which has previously been the dominant philosophy of most people associated with science, including social science.

This philosophy deserves brief consideration here for two reasons. First, existentialism exhibits many of the characteristics of a social movement itself currently on university campuses. As many people interpret it, existentialism reopens the question of the primacy of values over factual or epistemological concerns. It places greater emphasis on belief than on knowledge, on will than on logic, on normative judgments than on empirical verification. As employed by some, this argument skates very close to an out-and-out anti-intellectualism that asserts "what I feel is more important than what you reason." Seen in these terms, it becomes clearer why college revolts pit students against teachers, faculties against administrations, and large segments of the universities against the government in Washington. When people believe that they must stand up and be counted

4 R. L. Hamblin, "Leadership and Crises," Sociometry, 21, 1958, pp. 322-335.

they sometimes leap instead of looking. As one college president, Buell G. Gallagher, put it, the question is: "Can the heuristic controversy successfully contain the destructive forces of the eristic, or will the eristic pressures of our time reduce the campus to a brutal struggle for power?" [5] That is to say, can the organizations dedicated to the search for truth withstand the activities of those who pursue controversy mainly for the thrill of battle and the glory of victory.

Secondly, we may consider whether the underlying assertions of existentialism characterize social movements, apart from their content. Briefly put, are enthusiasm, dedication, and involvement necessary in a social movement? Many people think so, and certainly it is the expressive actions of the members that attract our attention to most movements. Some sociologists with whom I have discussed this situation feel that it is the messianic or millennial attitude that sets social movements apart from tamer kinds of voluntary organizations.

Without conclusive evidence, I tend to disagree. While a utopian dream fires many movements, it does not seem to me that this necessitates a particular manner. Within the last twenty years two movements in the arts—cool jazz and beat literature—have provided contradictory examples. The cool cats were certainly a movement by our previous definition, but they presented a *dégagé,* calm, almost somnambulistic appearance. The beats, on the other hand, ranged from "cool" to "hot" with a small number frantically trying to shock the rest of society. The earlier anarchists present the same spectrum—from individuals who sought to withdraw from contact with society to those who threw bombs.

In his study of voluntary organizations, Bernard Bar-

[5] Buell G. Gallagher, "Pressures, Priorities, and Process," in *Current Issues in Higher Education, 1965, Pressures and Priorities in Higher Education,* ed. G. Kerry Smith, Washington, D.C.: Association for Higher Education, 1965, pp. 55-62.

ber asserts that apathy characterizes most members.[6] The classic picture of the New England town meeting, with nearly total participation by the citizenry, Barber views as a myth created by Tocqueville and other contemporary writers, and believes that limited participation has always been with us. Evidence supports this view. Unions, churches, political parties, fraternities, the Veterans' organizations—all tend to develop a limited "élite" who run things for a complacent general membership.

Some observers argue that the waning of enthusiasm and development of stable institutional form is precisely the index of the end of the social movement. However, not every movement which "cools" solidifies, and conversely, some develop a tight structure while retaining considerable verve. This does not appear to be a simple question or one which can be resolved by appeal to definition.

Many groups, whether movements or other kinds of voluntary organizations, place great authority and trust in the leader. Barber notes some special problems which this poses. The leader who takes a job temporarily may find that no one else wants it, and may feel he must keep it for the good of the organization. Sometimes this may not be in his own interest, as when the doctor loses his professional skills while running the medical association. If the leader is convinced that the organization should be democratic, he may have trouble trying to lead people who want him to decide for them. On the other hand, elected officials may in time develop personal needs for re-election which block a democratic turnover. Some organizations, including governments, de-

[6] See: Bernard Barber, in Studies in Leadership: *Leadership and Democratic Action*, Alvin Gouldner, editor, New York: Harper and Brothers, 1950, pp. 477-504. Reference is made to Bernard Barber "Mass Apathy and Voluntary Social Participation in the United States" (Ph.D. dissertation, Harvard University, 1948).

velop a pattern of change in some offices and near life-
membership in others.

The long-term office may be at the top or only near it.
When the top office becomes long-term, dissident members may cry "oligarchy," and claim that elections are
rigged or pressured. Conversely, when the top office ro-
tates while some lower office becomes tenure-bound, the
cry may be raised that powers which are proper to the
top man are being usurped by his subordinate. In activist groups, holding one of the top jobs may disrupt a
man's family. He may simply "marry" the job and drop
his family almost altogether, or he may try to treat the
position as "just another job," in which case he risks replacement when a more eager applicant appears.

One cannot casually infer undemocratic policies and
intentions on the part of leaders merely because they
have been in charge for some time. Tenure may occur by
default of the "active" membership; it may indicate a
devotion by the leader who thereby gains loyalty expressed in repeated election to office; it may result from
the special technical demands of the job which make it
foolhardy and irrational to replace the experienced man
with someone who then must learn these special techniques; and it may of course actually represent what it
casually suggests, a monopoly of power by a small elite.

Thus, the question of engagement appears to be
threefold: Is engagement necessary for all social movements? If it is necessary, is it necessary for all members,
or only for the leaders? And, if engagement is necessary,
is it necessary for all time?

The Importance of the Movement in Society

After a movement has been described there remains the
question of its social and psychological importance.
That is to say, the questions of establishing events and
of evaluating them are separate. Alfred McClung Lee

once suggested that scientific curiosity could essentially be reduced to two basic questions: "oh, yeah?" and "so what?" [7] It is with the "so what?" that evaluation is concerned.

Each individual member evaluates the movement in order to decide whether to continue his membership, but if the social movement affects only the members themselves, evaluation by outsiders is more academic than practical. However, many movements have consequences for people who are not members, even for the whole society. Assessment and prediction of these consequences are important.

Evaluation is easier after the movement is dead, but it may be more important while it is living. How can we evaluate a movement while it still exists?

Newspapers and other mass media can be examined to see how much space is devoted to the movement, and a rough "content analysis" made to determine how much is favorable and how much unfavorable in tone. People from various walks of life can be asked to evaluate the movement in relation to others. This "reputational" study may even provide a sort of "sociometric" of social movements.

Political power may be indicated to some extent by voting strength, whether votes which have already been cast or votes which "potentially" may be martialled to decide some future issue. Money too is an index of much activity in our society, so an accurate financial statement tells us something about the power of a movement to act. Also, as noted earlier, where there is a complex division of labor and the functions of various units are closely interrelated, minor roles may carry great nuisance value, which may reveal some of a movement's potential bargaining power.

However, we should remember that the word "poten-

[7] Alfred McClung Lee, "Can the Individual Protect Himself Against Propaganda Not In His Interest?" Social Forces, XXXIX, 1, October, 1950, pp. 56-61.

tial" generally carries a concealed prediction. We can never really measure a potential of any sort. The best we can do is observe what occurs when some of the energy becomes kinetic and estimate the result were all of it so expended, or else make statistical inferences about it from previous occurrences. Thus judgments about potential voting strength, potential buying power, or other potentialities will probably remain at the level of a best guess and should be modestly identified as such.

Many movements are closely related to a few other movements, agencies, institutions, or social groups. Although their influence may spread subtly throughout society, their impact of help or harm will be greatest in a few places. To estimate probable effects, on the one hand, and to discover sources of support or opposition, on the other, we should look for alliances and target groups. Sometimes we can learn a great deal about a movement by cataloging its enemies. They may sense its threat before we do and arise to combat it, or there may be a symbolic clash in which one or the other has selected a convenient scapegoat. Other possibilities were mentioned in connection with coalitions. For numerous reasons preparing a roster of the special friends and foes of the movement may be enlightening.

When opportunities arise for a movement to cooperate with other movements or other persons who share some of the same interests, we can sometimes question whether the movement promotes only its own immediate interests or serves others. Non-cooperation sometimes means that a movement has become mainly the means of self-enhancement for its leaders, rather than the instrument of its stated purposes. Some leaders become so ego-involved in their work that what they are doing becomes less important to them than the fact that they are doing it. Seeing the movement as the extension of their own personalities, they may even defeat it themselves by refusing to ally with others who could help them achieve their stated objectives, lest they share credit and dilute the glory. (This pattern seems especially likely in perfectionist cults.)

Although operationally we might regard success in the major stated objective as our best criterion for the importance of a movement, this may not be the case. The various anti-drinking or prohibition movements illustrate the point. After separateness and bickering, they combined forces and succeeded in getting the famous 18th Amendment passed. This, nominally, was a success. However, enforcement proved difficult, public sentiment variable, and unintentionally prohibition abetted the development of gangster empires. The amendment was repealed, but the incidental damage could not so readily be undone. Most social scientists would probably judge that the nation was worse off for having had it, but this itself is hard to prove. The "Roaring Twenties" might have been just as bad with wide-open saloons. Anyhow, as a result, Prohibition has lost hold on most of the middle-class "respectable" citizenry and the movements that sponsored it are now generally repudiated. Systematically sorting out their success from their failures, the intended from the unintended consequences, the symbolic functions from the practical political power —these are difficult problems.[8]

Theory

We may conclude by redirecting attention to the most important scientific task, the development of a theory of social movements. Norwood Russell Hanson has stated the general problem well:

What is it to supply a theory? It is to offer an intelligible, systematic, conceptual pattern for the observed data. The value of this pattern lies in its capacity to unite phenomena

[8] An essential study in this connection is: Joseph R. Gusfield, "Social Structure and Moral Reform: A Study of the Woman's Christian Temperance Union," *American Journal of Sociology*, 61, 1955, pp. 221-232.

which, without the theory, are either surprising, anomalous, or wholly unnoticed.[9]

Do we now have a theory of social movements? There have been many attempts to theorize about certain kinds of common events, and a few writers have attempted unified theories with broad application. However, it would appear that today only the bold or uninformed would offer a complete and unified theory of social movements, or indeed any kind of theory which is more than the description of alternative processes and some of their associated consequences.

But even if we are not yet prepared to advance a comprehensive theory of social movements, we can at least note some requirements which such a theory should meet.

First, a theory of social movements should be interdisciplinary in the best sense of that word. Although social movements have been studied by psychologists, social psychologists, sociologists, anthropologists, historians, political scientists, economists, dramatists, poets, theologians, journalists and others, no single frame of reference or single discipline can provide answers to important questions which arise in studying social movements.[10]

The reason for this lies partly in the nature of modern scientific thought and partly in the nature of the phenomenon.[11] Much of our modern thought is organized in

[9] Norwood Russell Hanson, *Patterns of Discovery*, New York: Cambridge University Press, 1958, p. 121.

[10] Two books by poets are: Marguerite Young, *Angel in the Forest*, New York: Reynal and Hitchcock, 1945, and Langston Hughes, *Fight for Freedom: The Story of the NAACP*, New York: Berkley Publishing Corporation, 1962. For a broad scale view of social movements by a historian, consult: Vernon Louis Parrington, *American Dreams*, New York: Russell and Russell, 1964.

[11] For the reader seriously interested in the problems of theory building, an understanding of the neo-positivist position is essential. A good single volume is Herbert Feigl and May Brodbeck, *Readings in the Philosophy of Science*, New York: Appleton, Century, Crofts, 1953.

dichotomies. Freedom and order, statics and dynamics, organization and disorganization, individual and group, and so on. These rubrics, and others like them have served well to order our previous dialogues with nature but they all suffer a common limitation. Under the exclusion principle phemomena must be classified as the one thing or the other. However, social movements strongly resist this kind of classification. They lie on both sides of many dichotomies, and bridge the gaps in between.

A single social movement may be a different kind of phenomenon to different observers, and to variously different people in it, and moreover it changes over time. Consequently a somewhat different series of questions present themselves to scholars from the various disciplines, and the answers to some become the data for others.

Psychologists have explored the personalities of leaders in social movements, such as the Nazi party.[12] Social psychologists have examined crowd behavior, symbolic interaction, phenomena of persuasion, and small group behavior or "group dynamics." Sociologists have sought demographic and ecological variables underlying the rise of movements, and have tried to link them to studies of other kinds of organization such as religious denominations and political parties. Political scientists have looked at social movements as the source of reforms in decadent political structures, as the check on the monopoly of power by the large patronage parties, and as the incipient stage of new parties. Anthropologists have seen in them a reaction to the culture conflicts brought about when Europeans invaded American Indian and Oceanic populations.[13] Historians and journalists seem especially to have been interested in the

[12] For example: G. M. Gilbert, *The Psychology of Dictatorship*, New York: Ronald Press, 1950.

[13] In this context: see anthropological descriptions of the Ghost Dance and the Cargo Cults, nativistic religious movements produced, but not fostered, by white man's contact.

Utopian communities,[14] and certainly one attraction in studying social movements is to marvel at the peculiar ideologies and forms of behavior some men can devise.

As no particular discipline can now claim the study of social movements as its registered specialty, we may properly abjure the technical language of sociology to ask in the simplest terms the kinds of questions which a comprehensive theory may be expected to meet.

What is the previous condition of society from which a movement emerges? What sequence of events is required before a movement begins? What determines the timing of its inception? What are the personal characteristics of people which make them receptive to a new movement?

Why do some people join and others abstain? Once they have joined, why do people stay or leave? What determines who shall lead, and how? How does membership affect the member both within and without the movement? How does the existence of the movement affect people outside of it, and existing societal institutions? What external forces influence the movement or its members? How does the movement relate to other movements? What is the relationship between the things a movement stands for and the things it stands against? How do its adopted means relate to its stated ends? What groups in society stand to benefit should it assume power? What "social problems" would it solve and what would it create?

If a movement is over and seems to have succeeded, a good theory should explain the success. Was the time or milieu for some reason favorable? How did the movement attract and hold sufficient followers? What critical decisions were made? How did they manage to time their actions well?

If the movement has failed, a different, but similar series of questions are in order. Were specific errors made? Did the leader take a wrong road or wander into

[14] See, e.g., Arthur Eugene Bestor, Jr., *Backwoods Utopias*. Philadelphia: University of Pennsylvania Press, 1950.

a cul-de-sac? Why were numbers too few? Did they recruit an ineffective category of people when better ones were available? Did their form of organization handicap their work? Were they profligate of energy, winning skirmishes at the expense of the campaign? Did some clique pervert the movement to contrary ends? Did some other agency more effectively meet the need? Or did the movement pursue needs most people do not feel, or champion causes so bizarre that they could not fit the present population or the existing culture?

To summarize broadly, a complete theory should answer such questions as how the form of social action is related to the rationale and the purpose, whether under given circumstances a movement may be expected at all, and if one is indicated what determines when it will appear and whether it will flourish.

A few of these questions may have been answered, tentatively, in this study. More perhaps have been answered by other authors. Most require further research and more perceptive thought. Hopefully some of the needed theory will be provided by the readers of this book, themselves.

For many reasons and for some time to come, in Western society and in the emerging nations as well, we may expect that men will continue to band together in large numbers attempting to change portions of their culture and make alterations in their social order. And though we cannot fully describe these movements or predict with certainty what their effects will be, we may with profit continue to study them.

SUGGESTED READINGS

There is by now a very large literature about social movements, most of it written over a period of about three centuries and running perhaps to thousands of volumes. Hundreds of volumes have been written, for example, about the Communist and Nazi movements alone. Accordingly, nothing like a "complete" bibliography can be attempted. For further reading two groups of works are suggested here. The first is a representative list of textbooks, with some indication of the special features of each. The second is a list of works about specific social movements, chosen both to exemplify a rather wide range and for readability.

Texts

Cantril, Hadley, *The Psychology of Social Movements*, New York: John Wiley and Sons, Inc., 1941. Discussion of motivation and sketches of four movements—Oxford Group, Townsend Plan, Father Divine, Nazi Party.

Greer, Thomas H., *American Social Reform Movements*, New York: Prentice-Hall, 1949. Agricultural movements, labor movements with reference to the progressive party (La Follette) and the New Deal. Largely historical.

Heberle, Rudolf, *Social Movements*, New York: Appleton-Century-Crofts, Inc., 1951. Specifically concerned with the question of political parties and political order.

King, C. Wendell, *Social Movements in the United States*,

New York: A Random House Study in Sociology, 1956.
A brief synoptic discussion emphasizing the "career patterns" of movements, or phases of development.

Laidler, Harry W., *Social-Economic Movements,* London:
Routledge and Kegan Paul, 1953. Utopias from Plato to
the 1950's with major emphasis on socialism and communism. Extensive bibliography.

Nordskog, John Eric, *Contemporary Social Reform Movements,* New York: Charles Scribner's Sons, 1954. A collection of readings by forty-six authors on diverse subjects related to movements. Large bibliography.

Smelser, Neil S., *Theory of Collective Behavior,* London:
Routledge and Kegan Paul, 1962. Distinguishes Norm-oriented and Value-oriented movements. Large bibliography.

Turner, Ralph, and Killian, Lewis M., *Collective Behavior,*
Englewood Cliffs, N. J.: Prentice-Hall, Inc., 1957. Treats
movements within a more general context. Annotated
bibliography.

Accounts of Specific Social Movements

Anderson, Nels, *Desert Saints,* Chicago: University of Chicago Press, 1942. (Mormons.)

Asbury, Herbert, *The Great Illusion: An Informal History
of Prohibition,* Garden City: Doubleday and Co., Inc.,
1950.

Becker, Howard, *German Youth: Bond or Free,* New York:
Oxford University Press, 1946.

Braden, Charles S., *These Also Believe,* New York: The
Macmillan Co., 1949. (Various small religious sects and
cults.)

Chaplin, R., *Wobbly: the Rough and Tumble Story of an
American Radical,* Chicago: University of Chicago Press,
1948. (Industrial Workers of the World)

Cronon, Edmund David, *Black Moses,* Madison, Wisconsin:
University of Wisconsin Press, 1944. (Marcus Garvey's
"Back to Africa" movement)

Eister, Allan W., *Drawing Room Conversion,* Durham, N.C.: Duke University, 1950. (The Oxford Group Movement)

Fremantle, Anne, *This Little Band of Prophets,* New York: New American Library, 1960. (The British Fabian socialists)

Harris, Sara, *Father Divine: Holy Husband,* Garden City, New York: Doubleday and Co., 1953.

Horn, Stanley F., *Invisible Empire—The Story of the Ku Klux Klan—1866-1871,* Boston: Houghton-Mifflin Company, 1939.

Joll, James, *The Anarchists,* London: Eyre and Spottiswoode, 1964.

Lincoln, Eric C., *The Black Muslims in America,* Boston: Beacon Press, 1961.

Mugglebee, Ruth, *Father Coughlin of the Shrine of the Little Flower,* Boston: L. C. Page & Co., 1933.

Nordhoff, Charles, *The Communistic Societies of the United States,* New York: Hillary House, 1960. (A classic report on Harmony, Amana, the Shakers, Oneida and others. First published 1875.)

Parker, Robert Allerton, *A Yankee Saint,* New York: G. P. Putnam's Sons, 1935. (The Oneida Community)

Shannon, David, *The Decline of American Communism,* New York: Harcourt, Brace and Company, 1959. (This is one volume of a series edited by Clinton Rossiter, Communism in American Life. Others are noted in Chapter II.)

Stroup, Herbert Hewitt, *The Jehovah's Witnesses,* New York: Columbia University Press, 1945.

Taylor, Carl C., *The Farmer's Movement, 1620-1920,* New York: American Book Company, 1953.

Young, Kimball, *Isn't One Wife Enough?,* New York: Holt, Rinehart, and Winston, Inc., 1954. (Mormons)

Index

DATE DUE

OCT 20 '71	OCT 7 '71		
NOV 16 '72	NOV 16 '72		
DEC 12 '72	DEC 12 '72		
SEP 19 '73	SEP 18 '73		
APR 3 '75	MAY 2 '75		
GAYLORD			PRINTED IN U.S.A.